105

in **DETAIL** Interior Spaces

in **DETAIL**

Interior Spaces
Space · Light · Materials

Christian Schittich (Ed.)

Edition DETAIL – Institut für internationale
Architektur-Dokumentation GmbH & Co. KG
München

Birkhäuser – Publishers for Architecture
Basel · Boston · Berlin

Editor: Christian Schittich
Co-Editor: Andrea Wiegelmann
Editorial services: Sabine Drey, Ingrid Geisel, Thomas Madlener
Translation (German/English): Elizabeth Schwaiger,
Michael Robinson, Peter Green
Drawings: Kathrin Draeger, Marion Griese, Oliver Katzauer,
Emese Köszegi, Elli Krammer, Peter Lingenfelser, Andrea Saiko
DTP: Peter Gensmantel, Cornelia Kohn,
Andrea Linke, Roswitha Siegler

This book is a cooperation between
DETAIL – Review of Architecture and
Birkhäuser – Publishers for Architecture

A CIP catalogue record for this book is available from the
Library of Congress, Washington D.C., USA
Die Deutsche Bibliothek – CIP-Einheitsaufnahme
In detail: interior spaces: space, light, materials/Institut für
internationale Architektur-Dokumentation GmbH & Co. KG, München.
Christian Schittich (ed.). [Transl. from German to Engl.: Elizabeth Schwaiger,
Michael Robinson, Peter Green]. – München: Ed. Detail; Basel; Boston;
Berlin: Birkhäuser, 2002
Dt. Ausg. u.d.T.: Im Detail: Innenräume
ISBN 3-7643-6630-3

Printed on acid-free paper produced from chlorine-free pulp (TCF ∞).

Printed in Germany
by Kösel GmbH & Co. KG, Kempten

ISBN 3-7643-6630-3

9 8 7 6 5 4 3 2 1

Contents

Space, Light and Material: Concepts for Interior Design

Christian Schittich

From austere meditation rooms to mega-size, shrill shopping malls: the spectrum of interior spaces is vast. And there are just as many design concepts as there are tasks. Interiors, one could say, are the principal purpose of architecture. While the building skin offers protection from external influences, the interior is where people dwell – for living and working, for prayer, shopping or leisure activities. Interiors can be hermetically closed off from the outside, relinquishing all connections to the outside; they can even be subterranean. But they can open towards the outside and transition smoothly into the exterior space.

It is important to differentiate between creating space and creating interiors. Ideally, although this is rare, an architect designs both. Sometimes the architecture dominates the character of the interior so decisively through the surfaces of the building materials or the lighting scheme, for example in Ando's or Le Corbusier's alluring church buildings, that the interior work is delegated to the background and has little influence on the atmosphere.

Architects are often asked to design a pre-determined space. This task may apply to new buildings, but it is frequently related to conversions or upgrades of existing structures, for interiors are generally less long-lived than the buildings themselves. This is especially true in the area of consumer environments, that is retail stores and restaurants. These spaces are defined by fast-paced change and fashions tend to follow one another in rapid succession. Working with an existing space can be just as exciting as designing an entirely new space: in working with heritage protected buildings, for example, where the existing fabric has to be taken into account. The allure lies in staging the contrast between old and new and to tap into the charm of the existing building elements. The fairly neutral conditions of a retail store offer an entirely different point of departure: these spaces are intrinsically transitory and they allow architects and designers more room for play and experimentation, for unconventional approaches.

Aside from the space itself, the choice of materials for walls, floors, ceilings and furniture play an essential role in interior design. Their surface, texture and colour have a decisive impact on the atmosphere of the space. In contrast to the facade, users come into direct contact with the materials in the interior. They can look at them closely, touch them, feel and perhaps even smell them. The third decisive factor is light, regardless whether it is natural or artificial in origin. It can animate the inanimate and breathe life into the interior. The approach to light is a reflection of different require-

ments: at times, rooms are evenly lit; in other instances light is employed to "paint" three-dimensional figures to evoke sensual effects. After a minimalist phase in the 1990s, when the principal aim in the design of stores or designer apartments (often pursued at considerable cost and effort) was to achieve a reduction to the absolute essential, complexity and multiplicity have made a come back in recent times. There is renewed joy in colour and varied form, and even ornamentation has re-emerged. Experiential environments are sought after today, especially in the consumer sector. And major fashion houses have discovered that architecture can not only play an important role in forming a corporate identity but inspire media interest provided it is spectacular enough, becoming an important advertising factor. Thus internationally renowned architecture firms are commissioned to design the flagship stores, guaranteeing world-wide attention.

This volume presents the multitude of different tasks, concepts and materials employed to design interiors. The international examples range from a fashionable bar to an elegant concert hall, from a simple apartment to an extravagant boutique. Despite the creative variety, all these projects share what one might describe as a common modern philosophy. It is expressed in fine detailing as well as in the desire to find an appropriate design solution for each task in the search for true quality. We deliberately chose not to include projects where this "quality" consists mainly in superficial glamour.

1.2

Living Spaces

While it is standard practice to consult an architect or designer for most interior work, this is the exception rather than the rule in homes. There are few private clients who commission an architect to design their homes – and even fewer when it comes to consulting an expert on the question of interior design. This is especially true for existing homes. Financial concerns alone offer only a partial explanation. The principal reasons lie in attitude and taste: for most people, the home (be it apartment or house) is a private space, a retreat. We prefer not to let anyone else interfere with our choices. Moreover, this is the last frontier, so to speak, for a truly modern sensibility. It comes as no surprise, therefore, that many avant-garde homes are designed by architects for themselves (or for artists or clients who work in the cultural sphere). Architects have always looked to their private spaces as a means to translate their personal ideas into reality and to experiment – a trademark statement or even a manifesto. This is true for John Pawson, who took minimalism to its extreme in his 1999 design for his private house, an attractive older building in London (fig. 1.2). Fine materials, perfect execution, and the character of the walls and surfaces define the image of the interior: the architecture is reduced to its basic elements of space, light and materiel. Each additional piece of furniture, every picture on the wall would be superfluous or even distracting. Yet few people can afford minimalism in the style of Pawson! Not everyone has so much space that everyday objects can be locked away in carefully integrated built-in cupboards. The same applies to Maya Lin's introverted apartment for a software entrepreneur and art collector in New York (see pp. 56ff.). Although equally reductionist, the effect is entirely different. While white walls dominate Pawson's design, this interior is defined by light maple panelling (with minimal details): stairs and dividing walls, sliding- and revolving doors, the built-in kitchen. The dining table (fig. 1.3, 1.4) also fits into this category, with chairs that slide beneath the table to form a solid cuboid whenever it is not in use. The kitchen stools are integrated into the counter corners in the same manner. The result is a fascinating spatial puzzle, a graphic play of vertical and horizontal planes.

Sacred Spaces

Sacred spaces pose one of the greatest challenges to architects, for like few other building tasks they offer an opportunity to abandon purpose-oriented thinking and to create true space: space that is characterized by the interplay and material qualities of its enclosures and by how light is directed. Sacred spaces must evoke moods, be unique in their function and have symbolic content. Tadao Ando succeeded in meeting this challenge with simple yet expressive means in his prayer- and meditation room for the UNESCO in Paris (1995; fig. 1.5), a space for people from around the globe, of all races and religions. Ando's solution is a simple cylinder in exposed concrete, whose curved walls are articulated only by the formwork joints and the drill holes. On the granite floor, laid out in a pattern that radiates from the centre, there is but a single chair and light – light falling through the openings at the entrance, light from above that flows down the walls. The ceiling consists of a concrete disk whose diameter is slightly smaller than the circumference of the cylinder and which is suspended,

1.3   1.4

1.5

cross-like, at only four points. Despite, or perhaps because of this extreme reduction, Ando achieves the desired symbolic energy: believers from all world religions can discover references to their own faith in the concept and the design. The Finnish architect Juha Leiviskä also values the play with light in his church buildings, going so far as to regard it as the most important building material, even more important than brick or wood. Staggered wall panels through whose glazed interstitial spaces the flat northern light can penetrate into the fabric are typical of Leiviskä's architecture. The church and adjacent manse in Kupio, Finland (1992, fig. 1.1), are compelling proof of his ability to create cinematic lighting effects at different times of day and in each season. He makes clever use of the contrast between reflected, warm light and direct lighting. The indirect light on the walls behind the altar increases in intensity as the day advances and is at its strongest shortly before noon as the service draws to an end; later still, when sunlight penetrates directly into the space, it erupts into a symphony of light and shade. The new synagogue in Dresden by Wandel, Hofer, Lorch and Hirsch (see pp. 70ff.) is a contrast to the two buildings by Ando and Leiviskä. A tent-like structure of metal mesh is suspended into the "container-like" principal space creating a diffused, mystical light mood. There is no pathos in how the light penetrates into the room; instead it flows evenly from all sides. And while the furniture in Ando's and Leiviskä's interiors is so minimal that they derive their character entirely from the quality of the spatial design, the atmosphere in this church is strongly determined by exquisitely crafted "furniture sculptures".

Retail Spaces

Design can often depart in more daring and irreverent directions when architecture becomes a tool to seduce consumers into buying. For rapid change is king when it comes to the interior design of retail spaces. By definition the designs have a relatively short "sell-by date" and are therefore allowed to be more fashionable, indeed they should be trendy. This in turn means greater freedom for the architects than in other projects, where longevity is desired. The architects at propeller z hope to create a direct link between fashion and interior design in their Boutique Gil on Mariahilferstraße in Vienna (see pp. 88ff.). They have created a largely transparent showroom, which cultivates and playfully stages the voyeuristic impulse. Walls and ceilings are covered in the same linoleum. The furnishings and dressing rooms are fashioned from moulded polyester components. In combination with the rounded transitions, especially between floors and walls, they produce a futuristic effect of having been cast from a single mould and a fashionable colour scheme. Industrial materials and surfaces enter into a dialogue rich in contrasts with the textures of the clothing on display.

Conversely, the jewellery boutique Schmuckgalerie Isabella Hund von Landau + Kindelbacher (see pp. 80ff.) opts for a severe, minimalist stance. The tiny ground-floor space in a post-war building is rationally divided by means of a few, thought-fully placed elements and the carefully arranged display of jewellery in glass showcases. This type of minimalism differs from boutique designs realized by Claudio Silvestrin (e.g. Armani, Paris, fig. 1.6) or John Pawson (Jigsaw, London 1996), with their almost excessive abun-

1.6

1.7

dance of space and demonstrative display of luxury. Overall, there is a movement away from such minimalist luxury stores, where the absence of superfluous elements draws the eye to a small selection of carefully staged merchandise. Today, the principal aim in retail settings is to employ architecture and interiors as media that communicate a particular lifestyle and to create specific moods. The architecture is part and parcel of the image the label sets out to project. This is especially true for the flagship stores of the major fashion chains and sporting goods manufacturers (e.g. Nike Town in New York), which act as marquees for the major labels at the most exclusive sites in metropolitan centres. No expense is spared in creating these interiors, and instead of interior designers the trend, increasingly, is to commission internationally renowned architecture firms such as OMA (Rem Koolhaas), Renzo Piano and Herzog & de Meuron. The young New York collective of architects ARO achieved a perfect translation of corporate identity with their concept for the Qiora Store for cosmetics giant Shiseido in Manhattan (see pp. 84ff.). The entire interior design, reductionist and uniform, is a transposition of the label into form and colour, and at the same time a reflection of the extravagantly styled bottles and containers of the Qiora series of products. With their store for Marni in London, Future Systems have created a spatial landscape in which the items of clothing are themselves an essential element in the composition (see pp. 92ff.): a kind of total work of art – the store as a large showcase, a theatre stage. Designer Rei Kawakubo has led the way in the flagship-store movement with the boutiques for her fashion label "Comme des Garçons" which she designs in collaboration with architect Takao Kawasaki and more recently also with Future Systems. The Japanese fashion designer was one of the first to shift the focus in the early 1980s from advantageous product presentation to a unique combination of architecture, design and art. Many of the more recent stores are designed almost exclusively to showcase the lifestyle associated with her fashion: thus, one of her new branches in Tokyo no longer displays any goods at all. Upon request from the customers, the sales personnel fetch the relevant items from the storeroom. Instead, the boutique serves as a gallery for photography, crafts and contemporary art. The Prada Store in New York by OMA, opened in early 2002, (Rem Koolhaas; fig. 1.7), also refuses the mandate of serving merely as a retail store in the conventional sense. Reminiscent of Rei Kawakubo's boutiques, the clothing for sale is mostly relegated to side zones or displayed in cages, which can be rolled away when they are no longer needed. The store can be fully transformed into a public space: performances are scheduled for every afternoon, and all sales activities are suspended during that time; additional events are planned for the evenings. The enormous amount of money that has been poured into the interior design of the two-storey boutique is justified as an investment in advertising. To Rem Koolhaas, working with consumer architecture is an important task. In his critical essays, most recently in the Harvard Design School Guide to Shopping, he denounces the style employed in shopping centres and malls as chaotic and sterile, and chastises other architects, among them the great masters Mies, Le Corbusier and Frank Lloyd Wright, for not having paid more attention to this field. Supermarkets are one outcome of this neglect. The suburban wastelands around large cities are littered with such plain crates devoid of windows, but invariably surrounded by vast parking lots: faceless, purely functional architecture, built entirely with profit in mind. Dominique Perrault's supermarket for the M-Preis chain in Wattens in the Tyrol (see pp. 96ff.) proves that it doesn't have to be this way: with a carefully detailed steel and glass construction, he has created a building that respects the landscape and nevertheless establishes a distinct presence. In the interior, large glazed openings and skylights allow for natural lighting, which – in combination with carefully designed details – promotes an attractive atmosphere. Department stores are usually as banal and sterile as supermarkets, although they tend to be more elaborate. The Galeries Lafayette in Berlin (1996; fig. 1.8) is a notable exception. Jean Nouvel draws his inspiration from the Parisian models of the late 19th century with their atria crowned by large glass cupolas. To Nouvel, the interior is an experiential environment. The large atrium with two diverging glass funnels (the upper funnel diminishes towards the top, the lower towards the bottom) is the main attraction. Reflections in slanted glass panes result in semi-transparency, creating a sophisticated interplay of the visible and the invisible.

1.8

Gastronomic Spaces
As in retail stores, the principal role of interiors in restaurants and cafés is to create an atmosphere and to establish a special mood. Exclusive restaurants lean towards conservative interiors but trend-setting venues showcase more fashionable and hence short-lived interiors. One of the most widely discussed designs in recent years is the bar by Diller + Scofidio in New York's Seagram Building (see pp. 106ff.): a composition of moulded plywood, flickering monitors and matte glass that corresponds ideally to contemporary tastes. Vegie-To-Go, a take-away restaurant in Tokyo by Klein Dytham (see pp. 100ff.), is equally trendy: an effective translation of a convincing concept with fairly simple means. The invigorating, bright green evokes "nature" and the plastic vegetable silhouettes fulfill the dual role of label and decorative graphic element.

Office Spaces
New information technologies and modified working concepts have led to a proliferation of different forms of organisation in office buildings: from private and open-plan offices to fully flexible office landscapes, which may encompass an entire building, for example in the designs of the Dutch group of architects MVRDV. Most office interiors, however, especially those designed for established firms, banks and insurance companies, are standardized and their furniture is supplied by system manufacturers. And there is another factor: office buildings are frequently investment objects. Clients are replaced by investors and mass-produced furniture is installed for the future users. Even when this is not the case, the layout of the interior and the interior furnishings are predetermined to conform to average user requirements. The situation is different, however, in the many Internet companies that are emerging virtually overnight: the order of the day in these companies is rapid change and this allows for fashionable design less geared towards longevity, similar to the aforementioned retail environments. And the economic constraints that accompany the foundation of new companies

1.9

1.10

also promote creativity. Original solutions, often realized with simple means, are found in the former industrial buildings and warehouses of San Francisco (fig. 1.9), New York or in the east of Berlin. The colourful interior creates an interesting contrast to the coarse appeal of the old utilitarian buildings. Aside from Internet companies, architecture offices or advertising agencies are often notable for unconventional designs. The KMS-advertising agency in Munich designed by tools.off and lynx.architecture (see pp.120ff.) is a recent example, where the new interiors with their distinctive material range of felt, rusted steel and exposed concrete contrast attractively with the carefully renovated truck maintenance depot from the 1920s. Frank O. Gehry has created one of the most exciting office building interiors in his DG-Bank project on Pariser Platz in Berlin (2001; fig. 1.10) by placing a glistening, metallic organic sculpture inside the rectangular atrium. A successful gesture of surprise, for the building's exterior – a rather sombre perforated natural stone facade – gives the visitor no indication of what he will discover on the inside.

Cultural Buildings
Cultural institutions are much more than purely utilitarian buildings: their role is to set architectural landmarks in a city. Naturally one of the design task is to do justice to the function of the building and to communicate this function on the exterior. At the same time, however, it should profile the cultural ambition of the city and become a tourist attraction. Buildings of this kind can become famous landmarks. Successful architectural solutions from the past include Utzon's Opera House in Sydney, Scharoun's Philharmonie in Berlin and Frank O. Gehry's Guggenheim Museum in Bilbao. Dominique Perrault's National Library in Paris (1996, see pp. 128ff.) is also first and foremost an architectural manifesto, symbolizing the supremacy of France, and then President Mitterrand, as leaders in culture. To realize the distinctive design of the building with its four glass corner towers, resembling open books, a variety of organisational and functional shortcomings were accepted – a decision that was widely criticized. These are conceptual problems, not shortcomings in the design or in the details. In the interior, Perrault and his partner Gaëlle Lauriot-Prévost achieved a total work of art on a scale that has become extremely rare today: the architects designed every interior element, from furniture (the tables and chairs are now being manufactured as a series) to light fixtures, to wall- and ceiling panels. The result is a successful combination of conventional and innovative materials where the warm wood hues of the furniture contrast with the cool metal mesh on walls and ceilings. Another prominent example is the Tate Modern in London (2000; see pp. 138ff.). Here an existing "landmark" of the city – a striking power station from 1945 – was reassigned to a new use: the breathtaking conversion and restoration by Herzog & de Meuron has transformed the Bankside Powerstation into a renowned museum for modern art. The overall impression is dominated by the rational design of the exhibition spaces that allow the works of art to come into their own and the theatrical staging of the former turbine hall. In the latter, cool neon strip lighting contrasts with the bolted steel construction of the original structure with a black paint finish – a symbol for the transition from the sooty machine age to the flickering era of information technologies. Concert halls and theatres are

among the most challenging design tasks, aesthetically and technically: they demand good acoustics, excellent views of the stage from all seats and the appropriate atmosphere. Some such buildings announce their function on the outside – we have already mentioned the works of Utzon and Scharoun. However, since these stages and halls are always lit with artificial light, these may also be pure interior spaces, in the most extreme case even subterranean halls, as is the case with the former Lingotto Fiat factory in Turin, whose underground level has been converted into a concert hall by Renzo Piano. The interior design is largely driven by considerations for acoustics, which call for broken rather than smooth enclosure surfaces. An interesting solution to this task is found in the new concert hall in Léon by Mansilla + Tuñón (2002; see pp.154ff.).

Transportation Buildings

Buildings for transportation are nodes in the world-wide transportation network: this is where we board cars, trains, boats or planes. The close link between architecture and technology determines the formal expression of these buildings whose interiors are often characterized by exposed load-bearing structures. And yet these large transportation buildings are more than purely functional buildings, but sites that have a very unique representational character. Some of the most remarkable examples of the genre were realized at the close of the 20th century as a result of successful collaborations between architects and engineers: London's Standsted terminal by Norman Foster (1991), Waterloo Station in London by Nicholas Grimshaw (1994; fig. see pp. 41ff.) and Kansai Airport near Osaka by Renzo Piano (1996; fig. 1.11). Aside from their stunning construction, these buildings are also notable for the carefully thought out and contemporary details of the interior design as a whole. Subway stations, too, are pure interior spaces, in that they are underground and have no relationship to the exterior. They are purpose buildings with predefined volumes, whose interiors are subject to strict technical guidelines and tight budgets. Two examples in Munich demonstrate that such stations need not be monotonous, despite these constraints. Both translate original concepts with simple and yet rigorous means: the "Am Moosfeld" station (see pp. 164ff.), where a huge red and silver-grey sign of the station name serves as the principal design element, and "Westfriedhof" station (see pp. 166ff.) where giant lanterns create a dynamic counterpoint to the otherwise bare space.

Figures
1.1   Männistö-Kirche, Kuopio, Juha Leiviskä 1992
1.2   House, London, John Pawson 1999
1.3   Apartment, New York, Maya Lin 1999, dining-table
1.4   Apartment, New York, Maya Lin 1999, dining-table
1.5   Prayer- and meditation room, Paris Tadao Ando 1995
1.6   Armani-Store, Milan, Claudio Silvestrin 2001
1.7   Prada-Store, New York, OMA/AMO (Rem Koolhaas) 2002
1.8   Galeries Lafayette, Berlin, Jean Nouvel 1996
1.9   barnesandnoble.com, New York, Andersen Architects 1998
1.10 DG-Bank, Berlin, Frank O. Gehry 2001
1.11 Kansai International Airport, Osaka, Renzo Piano 1996

1.11

The Architect as Designer of Space: Classic Modernism

Christoph Hölz, Munich

Henry van de Velde's Villa Esche in Chemnitz (1902/03) was reopened in the fall of 2001 after several years of restoration work. For the time being, this villa is the final project in a series of restorations of important 20th century houses. Several years ago, various villas and country homes were renovated and converted into museums, among them the Villa Savoye in Poissy near Paris by Le Corbusier (1928), the Villa Mairea in Noormarkku by Alvar Aalto (1939) and Fallingwater in Bear Run/Pennsylvania by Frank Lloyd Wright (1937). There is a growing trend towards expensive restorations of such classic homes, many of which had been substantially changed in the intervening years and were thought to be beyond repair. In the past three years alone, five additional prominent examples have risen like a phoenix from the ashes: two master buildings in Dessau designed by Walter Groius (1925/26), Müller House in Prague by Adolf Loos (1930), Schminke House in Löbau by Hans Scharoun (1933) and Sonneveld House in Rotterdam by Brinkman and van der Vlugt (1933). The war-damaged houses, subsequently subjected to conversions and new uses, had lost their original appearance early on and were only known from historic black-and-white images dating back to the time when they were first built. Now that rigorous renovation and extensive reconstruction has been completed, they can be experienced once again in their original form and colour. Houses like these are an opportunity to reconstruct the genesis of modern architecture; their interiors are exemplary models of individual interior design even today.

Elements of Interior Design

As the examples on the following pages will show, it is important to pay attention to several essential aspects in order to analyze the design of interior spaces and trace characteristic styles. Aside from the proverbial "four walls" that demarcate the space, determine the proportions and thus set the basic tenor of the effect, interiors are rendered experiential through the layout of the floor plan and the path through the building. For only in walking through them, can we experience rooms in all three dimensions. The question of the relationship between inside and outside is fundamental to this discussion, as is the relationship between the enclosed interior space and the exterior and how the space is lit from natural or artificial light sources. Colour scheme and material selection are the further determining factors in addition to these primary architectural conditions.

And finally, the furnishings complete the design of the interior space. The options for interior design are sheer endless – the history of architecture is full of overpowering impressions and sublime creations of space. A complete portrait of this evolution would go beyond the scope of this discussion. Instead, we will attempt to trace the evolution of a vocabulary of interior design that continues to be valid to this day by looking at exemplary models. Interior design in private homes of the first half of the 20th century seems especially well suited to this task. The emergence of a bourgeois art of building and interior design embarked on a victorious career circa 1800 that has never diminished since. Around 1900 there was a clear break in architecture and interior design with the Historicism that had reigned supreme until that time. Until the mid-20th century, the theoretic formation of Modernism is documented not least of all in the debate on residential building. The houses selected for this volume all date from the period between 1900 and 1940. They set standards and decisively influenced the subsequent evolution in this domain. Almost without exception, these houses are luxurious city residences and country villas, in which the goals of the architects as creators of a "total work of art" were expressed with particular clarity. Nevertheless, the ideas they postulate had far-reaching impact.

"Reasonable" Interiors: Henry van de Velde

The Belgian Henry van de Velde (1863–1957), who felt a close kinship to the British Arts and Crafts movement, instigated a fundamental reformation of crafts at the beginning of the 20th century. He transferred the principles of civil engineering to furniture design more rigorously than others and for this reason the chairs, which he designed for his own home "Bloemenwerd" in Uccle near Brussels in 1894, are often compared to the iron skeleton of the Eiffel Tower. The Villa Esche in Chemnitz was not only van de Velde's first building in Germany (1902/03), it was also the self-taught architect's first opportunity to translate his ideas of a "new style" onto a large scale in the form of a total work of art. He owed this opportunity to the support of his client and patron, hosiery manufacturer Herbert Eugen Esche, who was among van de Velde's first clients in Germany and had bought furniture based on his designs as early as 1900. Esche, who was interested in the modern movement as a whole, wanted to have "a house that is in harmony with the spirit of the furniture and other objects designed for it." The estate thrones high above the city nestled into extensive grounds that were also designed by van de Velde. A patio leads to the main entrance set into the east elevation of the villa. The entrance, however, does not open onto a magnificent foyer, but into a nondescript corridor that leads around a corner into the large stairwell atrium, the true heart of this house. The hexagonal, habitable atrium reaches all the way to the roof, terminating in a decorative skylight. It is notable for several distinctive features: comfortable furniture loosely placed throughout; a large stove encased in colour-glazed tiles; and most notably the massive, wooden staircase that leads up to a wrap-around gallery on the second floor. The family's living rooms and bedrooms are located off this gallery. Service and staff rooms, as well as the servants' stairs, are separate from the living areas on the north side of the villa. The grouping of work-, living-, music- and dining rooms also follows this conventional spatial distribution around the atrium on the ground floor. But van de Velde's true strength lies in his creative design vision. He called his simple designs with ornamental curlicues "reasonable". The dining room in the west section of the villa boasts a portrait gallery backed by polished mahogany and textile wall covering, evoking the tradition and history of the Esche family (fig. 2.4). Van de Velde has added a theatrical element with electric light fixtures: each painting is lit with two bulbs attached to elegantly curved copper rods – an unusual and elaborate presentation for the period. The simple elegance of the furniture provides the perfect counterbalance to the *gravitas* of the forebears on display, for example, the elegant chairs with open-worked back-rests inspired by the early classicist furniture designed by Thomas Chippendale. Van de Velde introduced bright accents in the adjoining salon or music room: light is the leitmotif, with white and gold dominating the colour scheme, culminating in a fantastically shaped chandelier of brilliant white stucco, polished brass and clusters of bright bulbs that resembles a gigantic piece of jewellery (fig. 2.3). For its time, circa 1903, the understated furniture in white polished lacquer was just as spectacular. And finally, van de Velde's combination of three floor-to-ceiling windows with French doors transforms the south-west corner of the room into an area that is practically fully glazed, achieving a programmatic opening of the house to air, sun and light – the keywords of the Reform Movement at the turn of the century.

Although the Villa Esche represents a synthesis of tradition and reform, past and present, its design cast away many of the conventions and preconceived tastes of the time.

Spatial Expansion through Iron and Glass: Victor Horta
The break with tradition provoked by the Reform Movement and Jugendstil around 1900 is immediately apparent when we compare Art Nouveau interiors with those defined by Historicism. Victor Horta (1861–1947) achieved in architecture what his compatriot van de Velde mastered so convincingly in furniture design and craftsmanship. More stringent in approach than van de Velde, Horta looked to the monumental iron structures of the mid-century for inspiration. In his designs for elegant houses commissioned by forward looking entrepreneurs and engineers with a background in the chemicals industry (Ernest Solvay, Camille Winssinger and Emil Tassel), all built in the spacious new neighbourhoods of the prospering Belgian capital Brussels, Horta had begun to achieve a stunning

2.2

symbiosis of material and form, construction and ornament, as early as 1893. These projects unabashedly featured iron as a new material for facades and interiors. This was a courageous approach, for while Horta's contemporaries were familiar with iron constructions from the monumental halls erected for world exhibitions, from shopping arcades, railway stations and greenhouses, the crude material was still considered taboo in residential construction. Horta realized the Hôtel Tassel (1895) on a site that was emblematic for his residential projects, an enclosed strip on a very narrow but deep plot. The plan is developed along a prominent central axis. Horta explodes this solid corset by negating conventional ideas on ground plans and a seductive lighting strategy that draws the visitor directly into the hall and thence upwards, towards the light, into the upper floors. Solid masonry for dividing walls is kept to a minimum in this house. The stairwell, reception- and living rooms are divided only by glazed doors, which creates the impression of a continuous flow from room to room, an effect that is visually expanded and enhanced by large mirrored surfaces. The light colour scheme from delicate ochre to vibrant orange-red avoids any heavy or oppressive feeling. Slender cast-iron girders, columns and sections are visible throughout the interior, proclaiming the laws of structural support and postulating the new technical options and their aesthetics. Horta elevated utilitarian form into artistic form. The metal columns assume plant-like shapes: the capitals resemble buds, the shafts are reminiscent of flower stems and the bases roots. As if in adherence to the laws of flora, the iron supports in the stairwell seem to grow towards the source of light at the top, where they merge into the filigree pattern of branches in the glazed skylight. The stair banister rises like shoots between the columns, combining into an agitated, fiery ornament that is mirrored in the murals and floor mosaics on the stairs and landings. Like liana the then modern gas lamps in high-polished copper and brass with their fragile, paper-thin glass lampshades resemble delicate calyxes suspended from the ceiling. It is surely no accident that the transparent stairwell widens into light-flooded winter gardens in the annex areas, such as here in the bel étage and on the upper floors, where Horta's botanical namesakes, exotic orchids and rare lilies bloom beneath potted palms.

"History alone was timely": Foundation Period Interiors
In Germany, Gottfried Semper's (1803–79) passionate rejection of glass- and iron architecture had prevented it from being adapted for private buildings and public monuments – to Semper the Crystal Palace in London was a "glass-covered vacuum", a non-architecture and he demanded that there should be "mass" in the art of building. His buildings and theoretic writings made Semper into the most important architect of Historicism. His projects in the style of the Italian High Renaissance became prototypes of their kind. The later director of the Austrian Museum for Art and Industry (today Museum for Applied Art) in Vienna, Jacob von Falke, described the key elements in interior design at the time in his monograph "Die Kunst im Hause" ("Art in the Home") in 1871: "We encounter a rich ceiling decorated with carved ornaments, gold leaf and frescoes, walls with carved or segmented wood panelling, covered in guilt leather wall coverings, wall-paper made of silk and velvet patterned with gold and silver, or *arrazzi* abounding

2.3

2.4

with figures and colours, moreover, frames that are often designed by the artists themselves surrounding the finest examples of easel painting, all complemented with cupboards, tables, drinks trolleys, beds, trunks displaying the best in woodcarving and inlay, light and heavy seating with abundant upholstery, heavy curtains in front of windows and doors and beds, tumbling down to the floor, tables and floors covered in the most exquisite Oriental fabrics and embroideries, all this in warm, rich colours and saturated, full hues. [...] incomparably rich, noble and elegant, comfortable and furnished with true artistic taste, that is how written records describe the apartments of those highly-educated people who lived with Raphael and Titian [...]". To live like Raphael and Titian was not only a model for interior decoration, it applied to the entire reform of living. It began with the painters Hans Makart (1840–84) in Vienna and Franz von Lenbach (1836–1904) in Munich, who set themselves up as modern princes of art. Their lavishly appointed salons and studios became favourites with the upper middle classes, who were only too ready to emulate the artistic style of living. However it would be a mistake to dismiss the historicistic and emphatically craft-oriented 19th century interiors as anachronistic and old-fashioned "costumes". This blind approach to history has obscured the view of an entire century and its art for far too long. History alone was thought to be timely – four generations reserved recognition exclusively for models of architecture and interior design that were legitimized by historic roots as adequate styles. At the same time, modern innovations in house technology and construction were emerging beneath the historicising surface. The Villa Hügel in Essen is exemplary in this regard. Constructed between 1869 and 1873, the house is the very prototype of a Foundation Period villa. The client, industry baron Alfred Krupp, stipulated that his home should be designed according to his own ideas of "comfort", which – in addition to luxurious appointments – he understood as being running warm and cold water, water closets, a ventilation system, central heating and modern communication systems (telegraphy).

Continuous Interior Space: Frank Lloyd Wright
Frank Lloyd Wright's (1867–1959) contributions to international architecture were like a stroke of liberation. Even prior to 1900 he championed to for the destruction of the cardboard house, the idea of the house as a "cardboard box" composed of four walls, a floor and a roof. Wright cleverly drew upon the myth of the American West when the task arose to formulate a genuine American architecture. His most important contribution to residential building came with the so-called Prairie Houses. The low, spreading buildings with cantilevered roofs established a new relationship to nature by fitting respectfully into the existing topography and vegetation of the site despite their considerable size. In 1902/03 Wright realized the Ward W. Willitts House in Highland Park/Illinois, a Chicago suburb. The cruciform, "windmill-like" plan allows the four wings of the house to stretch into the surroundings. One has a tangible sense of the expanse of the American prairies, obliterating any lingering memories of European density. The external generosity continues on the interior in a most agreeable manner. With the horizontal line dominating over the vertical, these interiors create a sense of tranquillity and focus that allows their inhabitants or visitors to take a deep

2.5

breath. By basing his ideas on function, Wright truly conquered space in an entirely new fashion: not a trace remained of symmetry or axis; instead there were walls that identified and accompanied the most comfortable route from one interior space into another. All Prairie Houses are centred on a large chimney and the sequence of spaces seems to flow naturally from this core: the plan unfolds in the most literal sense of the word. Wright relinquishes unnecessary changes in level, developing a flowing ground-floor transition from entrance- to living- to dining area (fig. 2.5) leading to a fully glazed front overlooking a large terrace, and followed by the housekeeping wing with a generous kitchen and storerooms. The living rooms are notable for their privacy and intimacy. This atmosphere is much helped by the colour-leaded glazing, which screen the view of the nature outside in many of Wright's houses and bathe the interior in a coloured, almost dim light. This "fading out" of the environment focuses our attention on the interior, on specific areas, for example the seating area in front of the chimney. The floor plan is rigorously adapted to the various functions of living, so much so that almost every piece of furniture is assigned a fixed place as the numerous pieces of built-in furniture illustrate. Indeed there are few moveable pieces of furniture and even those have an element of "fixedness" as in Wright's design for a dining table with lighting fixtures integrated into all four corners and chairs with extremely tall backs that demarcate the dining area as a room within the room. Wright designed practically all elements for the Prairie House interiors according to function, but also with a view to their significance in terms of content. The aforementioned central chimney plays a pivotal symbolic role: it is the very expression of the "hearth" and reminds us of a campfire. The imagery in his ornamentation is, on the other hand, for the most part derived from Native American art. The material preferences also reflect this commitment to history and the genius loci: walls in red brick and roughly hewn natural stone masonry are reminiscent of the unspoiled nature we associate with the prairies. Wood is another important symbol of the place in this land of endless forests. Wright used mostly native types of wood for wall panelling and built-in furniture, harmonizing the autumnal colouring that prevails in the Prairie Houses with the dominant red and browns of these woods. This earthy, rustic character combined with otherwise luxurious appointments makes Wright's Prairie Houses into a determinedly American architecture.

Straight Lines and Flawless Surfaces: De Stijl
The changes in the political, economic and social landscape after the First World War prepared the ground, especially in Europe, for the emergence of new artistic and design ideas that had been germinating for some time in obscurity. From 1919 onwards, for example, Expressionism exploded into an abundance of ideas, a flowering of architectonic fantasies and utopias. A far more innovative impulse, which opened up new perspectives for the architectural design of space, originated in Holland. In Leiden, the radical De Stijl movement had formed a group as early as 1917 around the painter and architect Theo van Doesburg, the trained carpenter Gerrit Rietveld and the painter Piet Mondrian. The first architectural highlight of the movement came with the completion of the Schroeder House in

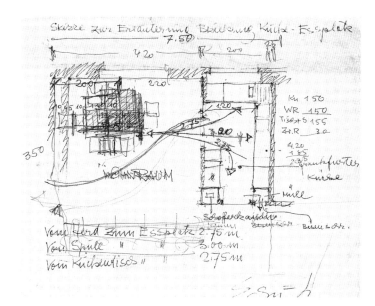

2.6

2.7

2.8

2.9

Utrecht, which Gerrit Rietveld designed in collaboration with his client Truus Schröder-Schräder. A lightweight steel skeleton enabled Rietveld to create a fluid spatial continuum, large windows and hence the desired abolition of boundaries between inside and outside. The cube shape of the house is divided into asymmetrical panes and solid surfaces, as is the case in the interior. The bedrooms on the upper floor are thrown together with the living area and only a system of moveable sliding walls transforms the large open space into small sleeping compartments at night (fig. 2.8, 2.9). The Schroeder House is an ideal translation of Mondrian's neo-sculptural style of composition (1914/17): straight lines and flawless surfaces intersect and penetrate at right angles and the primary colours red, blue and yellow are contrasted by white, black and grey. The interior is structured less by material surfaces than by colours. Thus a white field on the kitchen wall across from the ribbon window reflects the light that falls through the window back into the space, visually enlarging the room. Colours and light, built-in elements that complement the architectural composition – harmony reigns throughout. The design principle proved successful not only for the wooden, colour-lacquered built-in furniture but also in the construction of the famous "Red-Blue-chair", designed as early as 1918. It stands – as do other chairs and tables in the Schroeder House – as an "abstract-realistic sculpture in the interior of the future" to quote Rietveld. The simple gesture of introducing a diagonal into this system challenged the fundamental philosophy of the group and led to its dissolution. With Doesburg's death in 1931, the De-Stijl movement broke up for good. But its lasting influence on Mies van der Rohe, Walter Gropius and the Bauhaus would perpetuate important design principles.

New Interiors Suffused with Air, Light, and Sun:
Classic Modernism
Even before the First World War, many architects and architecture critics maintained that the most convincing applications of the "new style" occurred in industrial buildings. This impression was confirmed shortly before the outbreak of war at the Werkbund Exhibition in Cologne in 1914: aside from the theatre by Henry van de Velde, Walter Gropius's model factory and Bruno Taut's glasshouse were the most noted buildings at the exhibition. Younger architects like Mies van der Rohe from the generation born between 1880 and 1890 were convinced, however, that the innovations developed for utilitarian buildings would "truly come into their own not in industrial but in residential architecture". Plan and design of single-family houses and neighbourhoods borrowed from utilitarian buildings, proof of the architects' affinity with industry and technology, automobiles, aeroplanes, ocean liners and railways. The new guiding principles of typification, rationalization and standardization were derived from industrialization. The house should function like a "machine for living". The spatial economy and the rational approach to living were particularly evident in social housing and most of all in new kitchen designs. Margarete Schütte-Lihotzky, who was appointed to the Frankfurt department of building by Ernst May in 1926 to assist in the planning and realization of large housing projects, designed the radically minimal "Frankfurt kitchen" (fig. 2.7) in an effort to develop new, contemporary concepts for living. The forms and functions

of the kitchen were based on studies of movement: steps, hand movements and body rotations were to be reduced to a minimum and the paths shortened to create a design that would make housework into a simple and time-efficient task. This meant that each object had to be assigned a precise location. The placement of the working surfaces, their height and orientation to the kitchen window were also developed on the basis of these studies. The window itself had a raised sill to ensure that a breeze could flow into the room even when the counter was filled with objects. For artificial lighting, Schütte-Lihotzky designed lamps whose light cones were conceived to illuminate the breadth of the room at working level. Smooth surfaces and easy-cleaning metal drawers in the built-in cupboards promised a new level of hygiene: the floor was tiled, the kitchen furniture stood on a concave moulded base. The colour scheme also played an important role: "The colours fundamentally determine the correct distribution of the cubes and the incoming light [defines] the room proportions and hence the quality of the atmosphere in the room". The horizontal surfaces, including the floor, were kept in black, while the built-in furniture was finished in blue and the walls in ochre. Sinks, faucets, drawers and cupboard components were developed in collaboration with industry experts. For the Praunheim housing project in Frankfurt, limited editions of built-in furniture were manufactured from prefabricated industrial components. As for the building construction – the housing project is a panel construction – this method was aimed at lowering costs and making the apartments and kitchens affordable even to lower-income groups. Five kitchen models designed by Margarete Schütte-Lihotzky were presented in 1926 at the Frankfurt Exhibition on "The new apartment and interior finishing"; numerous national and international exhibitions (among others the Werkbund Exhibition in Stuttgart in 1927) followed and helped to promote the international recognition of the "Frankfurt kitchen". These design principles have influenced the concept of built-in kitchens to this day, although the components are developed independently of the spatial conditions.

Rationalized Living Space: Le Corbusier
Le Corbusier completed his series of villas near Paris with the Villa Savoye in Poissy (1931), a paradigmatic masterpiece of 1920s Rationalism and of "classic white modernism". But Le Corbusier (1887–1965) had already participated two years earlier in the Weissenhofsiedlung in Stuttgart with two houses, which exemplified his programmatic five points for a new architecture: *pilotis* or stilts that raise the building to first-floor level; roof gardens; open plans; open facades and ribbon or strip windows. The single-family house in Stuttgart based on Le Corbusier's "Citrohan" Houses (fig. 2.11) consists mainly of a large two-storey high living space and a large glazed south facade. Life in this space would unfold in an atmosphere of air, light and sun. The new lifestyle and body awareness is most ingeniously expressed in the generous roof garden, which provided space for exercise and sunbathing. Bedrooms and spare rooms are allocated to the rear of the house, like necessary "boxes" on a reduced plan. This rational approach to habitation is even more evident in the Stuttgart duplex whose interior Le Corbusier modelled on a railway sleeper. While this house also rises to a total height of three storeys topped by a roof garden, there is only one

2.10

main floor, which serves as a single large living- and sleeping area. Beds could be folded down at night and divisions created for "sleeping cabins". The minimal dimensions of the corridors, designed to the exact measurements of a railway sleeper, made conventional furnishings virtually impossible. The closets, simple wood constructions with sliding doors, were built-in. It is interesting to compare Le Corbusier's houses with Mies van der Rohe's: while the Frenchman had little interest in refined building materials – his preference was for white or tinted plaster, concrete slabs and prefabricated industrial products even for villas – Mies's architecture lives through the aura of luxurious semiprecious and high-grade natural stone, not least of all as a status symbols for his clients. Le Corbusier strove for new standards that would make cost-efficient building possible. To Mies such considerations were foreign.

Unlimited Living Space: Mies van der Rohe
Ludwig Mies van Rohe (1886–1969) created his two most notable masterpieces within a single year, in 1929/30, before he emigrated to the United States: the German Pavilion for the Barcelona Exhibition and Tugendhat House in Brünn (Brno). Mies had laid the ground for his novel spatial composition in two previous projects, a country house in reinforced concrete (1923) and a brick country house (1924). But with his pavilion for the 1929 World Exhibition in Barcelona, Mies went beyond his earlier designs in the simplification of the elements and the generosity of interpretation. Light, chromium-plated steel columns with cruciform cross-sections supported a reinforced concrete slab on a travertine base. Vertical travertine

2.11

and glass panels enclosed the covered area or penetrate through and beyond it. The orthogonal, asymmetric disposition of the wall surfaces achieved a flexible but defined order in the space without interrupting its flow. The original pavilion stood only for a few months. But all the essential compositional elements are still preserved in a house, which Mies designed during the same period in a completely different location in Europe for the Jewish textile manufacturer Fritz Tugendhat and his wife. On an exposed hill site in an upscale residential neighbourhood in Brünn (Brno) with a view of the Baroque fortress, the house takes one by surprise with its hermetic exterior and unusual spatial disposition. The ground floor, where the main entrance is located, houses the private study and bedrooms of the family. A staircase leads to the main floor below. Here the nearly 280-square-metre living area, including the east-facing winter garden, makes a spectacular impression. The room serves as the owner's study, reception-, library-, music-, dining- and living room in one. The most distinct space-dividing elements are two freestanding, non-structural walls – one in honey-coloured onyx and the other faced with red kusam panelling – while the chromium-plated load-bearing columns have no space-dividing impact. The furniture on the other hand is very much space defining. For the scattered seating groups and individual pieces, such as the wooden sideboard with zebrawood veneer or the round dining table anchored to the floor on a chrome column, are placed with precision. Nothing is left to chance. Almost all the pieces were custom designed for the house. The scale of the glazed wall was unprecedented. There were no more windows in

2.12

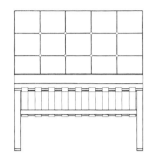

2.13

the conventional sense, the entire south- and east sides are "open" from floor to ceiling and offer a stunning view of the garden (fig. 2.14, 2.15). Other wall sections come alive entirely through their material: the library niche is fully panelled in kusam wood, the wall to the sideboard consists of white milk glass. This explains why there can be no paintings in this elegant room – the room itself is image enough. Tugendhat House was without equal not only aesthetically, but also in terms of technical-structural aspects, and in many respects it was even ahead of its time. The principal innovations were the continuous steel skeleton construction, the fully retractable, nearly 5-m-wide panes and the cleverly devised heating- and ventilation system. All these elements were prerequisites for exploding the conventional cubicle plan into freely interconnecting living areas with generous glazed external walls, which create a completely new relationship to the outside.

The "Spatial Plan": Adolf Loos
The Viennese architect Adolf Loos (1870–1933), nearly fifteen years older than his colleague, chose a different path, developing ideas on his own new architecture at the start of his career between 1900 and 1910. It was Loos's student Heinrich Kulka who gave it the name by which it is still known today in 1931: "spatial plan". According to this plan all rooms in a house would have the length, width and height that matched their function. The concept of continuous floors was almost completely abandoned: Loos connected the individual rooms in ascending sequences of movement based on the corresponding purpose of each space, allowing them to flow into one another. The height

differences between levels were overcome with a series of stairs. The sequential movement was deliberately orchestrated by means of material selection, guided direction and lighting. In 1922 Loos implemented his "spatial plan" for the first time in the Rufer House in Vienna. An even more artful and generous execution succeeded with the construction of a house for the affluent developer Frantisek Müller in Prague between 1928 and 1930. Although the house can be compared to Le Corbusier's in its radical nakedness, the interiors and spatial interpretation could hardly be more different. And although Loos shared a taste for precious materials, rare woods and natural stone with Mies, the differences between their buildings are greater than any commonality. Loos stated his programmatic intent as early as 1912: "The house should be secretive to the outside and reveal its full wealth on the inside" – a motto that is fully expressed for the first time on the second floor of the Villa Müller. Ascending the central stairs, one lands suddenly in a luxurious salon. The lighting design enhances this surprising scenario: to begin with a low, narrow ascent, the path leads into the wide, bright living area of the villa. The two-storey-high hall stretches along the full length of the garden front, with light flowing into the space through three tall windows. A brick fireplace attracts the eye between cipollino-clad columns on the narrow side of the room to the east, matched by a long, built-in bench between cipollino bases on the opposite end (fig. 2.10). To the left, a spiral staircase leads from the hall into a private boudoir. Here, Loos designed an intimate room, which contains a seating group that is fully integrated into the lemon-wood panelling. Stairs lead up to an intermediate landing followed by two

2.14

2.15

2.16

2.17

more steps up to the dining room, which overlooks the living room across a balustrade. Once again, Loos created an entirely different spatial impression: low room height, lateral lighting from a single window in the oriel, brown-red mahogany panelling on the walls and the ceiling generate a sense of containment. Despite the fascinating effect of each room and the dramatic visual links between them, Loos's "spatial plan" for the Villa Müller and other projects did not succeed as an established model: it was simply too expensive and moreover questionable in terms of functionality. (After all, who could cope with constantly walking up and down stairs with advancing age?)

Organic Spaces: Hans Scharoun
One of the most accomplished buildings of classic modernism in Germany was completed in 1933 shortly before the National Socialists seized power: Schminke House in Löbau, near the Polish border. In 1935 Julius Posener celebrated the house in his journal *"L'Architecture d'aujourd'hui"* as "one of the most subtle creations of our epoch" and the architect of the villa, Hans Scharoun (1893–1972) maintained even at the end of his long career that it was "the house I liked best". The Schminke House enabled Scharoun to realize his ideal vision of a single-family house and to build on his experiences gained, for example, at the Weissendorfsiedlung in Stuttgart in 1927. The following points were especially important to him: " [...] [a] clear separation of living-, sleeping- and service areas, [...] unifying [the] various functions of living into one spatial unit, [...] the play of the axis that leads through the entire house as a linear component versus space, [...] a form of living space that communicates a sense of expanse beyond the wall-like enclosure; [...] maximal integration of the [...] landscape". Scharoun made clever use of the ship metaphor and imbued the house with the character of a luxury yacht at anchor. In truth, this "ship" does not offer a conventional image to the observer, it has no identifiable face; instead, the visitor is set in motion and experiences the architecture through movement. There are as many visual axes between the spatial compartments in the interior and from the inside to the outside as there are positions one has to take in order to grasp the house in its entirety: a mostly harmonic, "organic" intertwining of interior and exterior (fig. 2.16). "Living in and with whatever weather conditions might arise" is how Scharoun and his clients, the industrialists Fritz and Charlotte Schminke, put it. The single-storey house consists of a single large room on the ground floor that serves various functions: thus the central, elongated living room, lit from the north and south side, transitions smoothly into the sunroom and winter garden to the east. Dining area, studio and entrance area, are lined up to the west. Only the service wing with "granny flat" for an employee lies separated from the living area behind an open staircase that leads in a wide curve upstairs to the bedrooms. But the various spaces on the ground floor are by no means treated in an "egalitarian" fashion: each section is assigned to a specific function and designed with differentiated materials, forms and colours. The ambience of the interiors was greatly defined by the colours chosen for wall- and ceiling surfaces, floors, furnishings and textiles. In addition to pure and off-whites and black, Scharoun set accents in silver, yellow, orange, red and blue; these colours were complemented by natural

NORDWESTSEITE

LÄNGSSCHNITT

materials such as walnut and oak, marble and rubber. Art and architecture critic Adolf Behne gave a detailed description in a contribution dedicated to the Schmincke House published in *"Innen-Dekoration"* in 1935: "Floor covering [in] dark blue velour, blue and grey rubber and Silesian marble with brown and black veins, [...] curtains [in] pastel yellow, [...] white metal handrails, [...] silver and black wall in the hallway, [...] white maple in-built wall closet upstairs." Scharoun championed a blend of natural- and artificial lighting. He developed a complex lighting system of wall and ceiling lamps, oscillating between a subtle play of light and perfectly staged lighting. The ground floor offers several surprisingly original solutions: the sunroom ceiling consists of a perforated metal surface through which fixtures mounted in the space between the metal plate and the ceiling above cast indirect light down into the room. The vestibule and the large living room are lit by spray-painted, two-armed candelabra, which cast their light up to the white ceiling whence it is reflected downward, while the dining area is suffused in daylight penetrating into the room through a ceiling perforated with glass prisms. Wall hangings and moveable room dividers made it easy to modify the spatial relationships and to give

2.18

the house, so open in daytime, a more intimate character at night. The furniture also reflects this differentiated approach to interior space: the living room is dominated by the several-metre-long, built-in upholstered sofa beneath the ribbon window, while the dining area and the sunroom are furnished with tubular steel pieces on parquet or marble floors to provide an hygienic, airy and light atmosphere. The question whether Schmincke House did not in fact offer too much space for play and openness was asked for good reason. At any rate, one is hard pressed to find protected, cosy nooks. In subsequent house designs, Scharoun revised this aspect and looked to Scandinavian models for inspiration.

"Natural" Space: Alvar Aalto

From the early 1930s onwards, important impulses for architecture, interior design and design came from Scandinavia. The national exhibition in Stockholm in 1930, where the full spectrum of New Building themes was presented, no doubt contributed to this sudden growth. A younger generation of architects, among them the Finn Alvar Aalto (1898–1976) and the Dane Arne Jacobsen (1902–71), began to combine modernism and tradition in

The Practice of Interior Finishing

Gerhard Landau and Ludwig Kindelbacher, Munich

Interiors are our daily living- and working environments. Interior design is not only a matter of function, but also of aesthetics and emotional comfort. Interiors should therefore successfully combine functionality and aesthetics and interior design or integrated spatial concepts are generally understood to fulfill both aspects. This does not, however, translate into an exclusive use of standardized industrial products or the addition of individual elements as decorative accessories to the architecture. Rather, the task is to develop a particular spatial concept for each individual design. Conventional spatial concepts and their traditional approach of allocating building components to specific uses have dulled our visual sense. Developing conceptual design ideas that can be implemented down to the finest detail is a completely different matter: finishing details, forms and materials serve as elements that support the design and not independent purposes, and the manner of their composition creates the interior space.

To begin with, the design and planning of interiors is subject to the same principles as building construction. However, since thermal and energy requirements play a subordinate role in interior works, they offer greater freedom in construction and a wider range of spatial design options. But there are additional requirements in terms of acoustics and lighting. The planning of interior spaces is determined by a multitude of predefined parameters: aside from the interpretation of the interfaces between inside and outside, the principal issues are user frequency and how usage duration is estimated. Building guidelines, codes, safety requirements and similar restrictions may also have considerable influence on how interiors are designed.

What follows is a detailed presentation of the various activities and tasks that are relevant for interior finishing, from conversion of existing spaces to the creation of new interiors. The technical requirements and the corresponding building components are explained. Examples demonstrate the functions and materials assigned to each component in special design concepts.

Working with Existing Structures –
Conversion and Refurbishment

Working with existing structures is without doubt one of the most frequent planning tasks. Tenant turnover, new uses, changes in the corporate image of firms, renovations and often simply the desire for change and refurbishment trigger commissions in this area. Precise analysis and evaluation of the existing spatial conditions is a prerequisite for successful planning. The envelope or building skin must also be analyzed with regard to existing structures. It is important to identify the load-bearing building components to form an image of the structural options. Unique features of the building or the rooms, for example the contact between interior and exterior, views, emission stress loads, natural lighting, natural ventilation, public and private areas all influence the design options and must be analyzed accordingly. It is also useful to clarify building restrictions before the planning begins to judge how much room for play there is and to co-ordinate the project plan. Assigning a space to new uses often requires permits and unexpected demands may arise when planning for interior renovations with regard to applications and authorization. Proof of parking or plans for landscape designs are frequently required by the relevant authorities as part of the application. Conservation guidelines also play a considerable role in conversion and renovation projects, where it may be necessary to collect permission from heritage protection authorities, deliver expert analyses of the existing fabric or restore the original condition of built-in units or building components. Here, familiarity with and expertise in historic building methods facilitate the work with the old substance. In more recent buildings it is important to check the fire safety codes and to integrate them into the planning if necessary. In multi-storey building the outline conditions for building systems, supply and disposal must be included. Planning and financial considerations are also affected by the issue of dealing with problem sites (asbestos, PCBs, etc.). The planner must take all these factors into consideration when evaluating the existing structural substance. At the same time, these factors impose definite challenges on the design. It is essential that the existing conditions (attached and non-attached built-in units, building component that cannot be removed, poor floor plans and room proportions) do not limit the design process. Constraints may in fact act as catalysts for interesting solutions: the implementation of unconventional ideas leads to spatial concepts that are tailor made for the specific situation, as is

3.2

3.3

the case in the interior work for a dentist's office (fig. 3.3). Figure 3.2 depicts the situation prior to renovation; the small rooms made natural lighting in the waiting area in the corridor impossible. Since the building dates from the 1950s and was realized as a steel skeleton construction with fairly large span widths, the existing dividing walls could be torn down, restructuring the interior into a generous spatial composition and moving the waiting area out of the hallway. Glass show-cases have been integrated into the room dividers between the access zone and the treatment rooms on the side facing the hallway, and these cases now house a small "museum of dentistry". The other side of the room dividers, facing the actual treatment rooms, contains the supply cupboards. Removable stainless steel panels provide easy access to the medical utensils stored inside these cupboards. Lighting and ventilation are integrated into the ceiling panel, set off from the existing ceiling by a distinct joint.

Another important aspect in planning work on existing buildings is project co-ordination. Factors such as construction work during continued operation or in cramped conditions, the needs of neighbours and protecting building components not affected by the new construction must all be taken into consideration and planned.

Interior Work in Connection with Planning New Buildings

Separate Planning Tasks for Construction and Interior Finishing
When construction and interior finishing are executed by different architects in new buildings, it is important to co-ordinate these tasks from the very beginning whenever possible. When the interior work is included in the overall building plan, special wishes and ideas can be taken into consideration for the ground plan and for components that cannot be changed after completion. Structural factors, for example, can be adapted and building code requirements taken into consideration. The interior finishes, specified in contractual agreements with investors or landlords, may have to be re-negotiated with future tenants. Absorption of costs should be discussed and agreed upon in detail.
Close co-ordination with the individual trades for the various building systems and the integration of the interior works into the schedule for the entire project open the doors for new design options and often simplify the planning. To avoid conflict during execution, the interfacing between the individual trades must be planned in detail and with implementable logic. Communication, participation in integrative planning meetings and the co-ordination of the wishes expressed by the users and the expert planners facilitate the entire course of the project. Additional synergies in terms of cost and scheduling can be achieved by contracting firms that are already involved in the construction. Integrated planning of construction and interior works is largely dependent on the readiness for co-operation on the part of the contracted architects.

Conceiving Buildings and Interiors "hand in hand"
Ideally, the architect is contracted for the total planning task for the building: this makes it possible to develop and implement design ideas without risk of running into the conflicts of interest mentioned above. It also allows for a rigorous realization of a total building concept from daylight deflection to lighting, building automation to building systems, and landscape design. Planning the interior works is

as much a part of the total planning as is the tender and contracting of special services; the aforementioned interfacing between trades can be centrally co-ordinated.

Building Components

Floors
Function: overlaying, installation carrier, heating, cooling, air conditioning, ventilation, cable systems, and zoning. Floor coverings should optimally fulfill the requirements in terms of function and design. In addition to frequency of use, the location within the building and the technical parameters are essential considerations. The latter include above all the sub-grade composition, requirements with regard to footfall and sound insulation, superstructure heights as well as transitions and links to the adjacent areas or building components. In the case of the bank branch for the Hypo-Vereinsbank on Marienplatz in Munich (fig. 3.14, see pp. 40ff.) the location and high frequency of use was an important consideration in choosing the floor covering. The choice was somewhat limited by the fact that the polygonal and diminishing conical shape of the plan did not allow for a unique, understated geometry and excluded natural stone as a flooring option. The homogeneous and jointless synthetic resin covering chosen for this interior enhances the design concept of the "internal arcade", while at the same time offering options for detail work on the stairs that bridge the existing difference in level. Risers and treads are covered in synthetic resin, allowing for a continuous flooring solution that does not interfere with the monolithic floor design. Lacquered MDF panels were used for the foldout strip at the base of the wall. The cable conduits behind this strip offer great flexibility for installing electric circuits and variable DP hook-ups throughout the ground floor.

As this example shows, when working with existing buildings it is important to realize that a variety of situations may exist that can limit the choice of flooring. Aside from problematic floor plans, difficulties may arise as a result of brittle or uneven existing finishes, surfaces that are difficult to treat such as planks, high absorbing or flaking cement floors or old floor coverings that cannot be removed.

Existing floor levels may further limit the options for resurfacing or new flooring, and difficulties in creating a smooth transition between the new floor and the surrounding surfaces must also be taken into account. If the existing floor surface can be fully removed, the options are more or less the same as those available to planners of new buildings. Ultimately the decision depends on the specific requirements:
selection criteria are drying time, bringing moisture into the building, cost, weight, sound- and thermal insulation requirements, as well as load capability and installation options.
The choice of top layer is also determined by these factors – terrazzo, for example, or a surface treated flooring material as in the case of the Hypo Vereinsbank.
Beyond these considerations, there are a number of additional factors, which have to be considered for the planning:
• the high temperatures that are generated when laying down asphaltic mastic and which must be considered for the installation of building systems close to the floor surface;
• the moisture sensitivity of the anhydride flooring;
• the disposition of flooring- and building joints;
• the compatibility of flooring and floor heating.

3.4

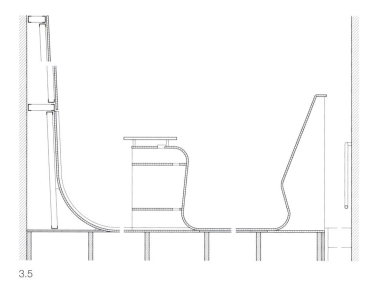

3.5

False- and hollow floors offer a high degree of flexibility and facilitate subsequent installation or upgrades of the technical services. It is important, however, to plan in advance for (future) installation of floor tanks, inspection and maintenance openings or false floor grids. The floor covering plays an important role in the room impression and it is therefore an essential design element; at the same time, the selection is dependent on the type and frequency of use, that is, the specific demands that are made on the floor. This means that aesthetic and practical requirements and the consideration of the floor plan determine the degree of shine or gloss, the joint pattern, joint width or absence of joints in the direction of the flooring is laid out, reflections (spotlights) or interaction with vertical building components (walls). The grey linoleum floor in the New York clothing boutique shown in figure 3.6 defines the atmosphere of the space. There is no differentiation between floor- and wall surface, cashier counter and banister are cut out from the grey area that is laid across the adjoining components like a second skin.
In public areas or medical facilities, additional technical characteristics must be considered in choosing the flooring aside from the aforementioned requirements.
Depending on the building task, these are:
• antiskid properties,
• conductibility and performance in case of fire,
• cleaning properties (type of cleaning, effort)
• dirt-repellent/dirt-absorbing,
• hygiene,
• durability,
• vapours, contaminants.

Last but not least, repair options should also be considered as a selection criterion.

Walls
Function: spatial enclosure, external/internal wall, load-bearing/non load-bearing, flexible, screening (sound, light, safety, radiation), transparent/translucent, installation carrier, facework, lining, functional unit (furniture), wall with bearing surfaces (fire protection etc.), light carrier, light deflection.

Existing Walls
Any design for work on existing buildings must begin with the analysis, i.e. the first step in the planning process is to establish the need for repair and restoration of walls that need to be integrated into the structural substance. The following paragraphs deal with some of the essential aspects, which may be important in this context: measures such as salting-out and dehydration, removing loose plaster, protecting or restoring old mouldings and surfaces or plaster repairs. In some cases it may necessary to expose the masonry or load-bearing structures such as framework. Moreover the options of surface treatment and the existing walls must be adapted to building codes and regional regulations.

New Walls
In new buildings the design of wall areas is primarily determined by the design-dependent decision for massive or lightweight construction. Massive construction offers the following traditional design options:
• Exposed masonry with a wide variety of materials and surfaces,
• Exposed concrete with a wide variety of formwork patterns:

3.6

Relief through formwork processing prior to pouring the concrete, surface treating after the concrete is poured (charring, granulating, etc.), and finally the various colourings that can be created by using a variety of additives and grain mixtures. Smooth or structured finishes and paint coatings can also be employed in massive construction methods. When using trowel-finishes or finishes with little grain, good preparation of the base and careful execution are vital, since spotlights expose any unevenness and smooth surfaces every crack. Glass fibre mats in combination with trowel finishing produces the desired surface quality. Paint coats can serve to achieve a wide range of designs and are available in any degree of gloss from matte to high gloss: the different techniques (stucco lustre, rub-on and wipe techniques, glazes, etc.), can be combined with the material properties of available plaster finishes to great effect.

In contrast to massive construction, lightweight walls – such as plasterboard or gypsum board walls – have the advantage of less weight as well as offering more flexibility and easy disassembly. They can meet the same design and technical demands as massive, plaster or speckle finished walls. For interior walls that need to fulfill only minimal technical requirements, there are nearly unlimited options for design. Individual pieces of furniture can also be utilized as room dividers or folding-, hinged-, sliding- or shutter walls can be used to create mobile wall elements. These can be manufactured out of transparent, semi-transparent or diaphanous materials (glass, plastics, fabrics, mesh, perforated sheeting, and lattice).
The cosmetics store shown on page 84ff. is divided into sections by floor-to-ceiling, diaphanous organza panels suspended from the ceiling, whose undulating outlines underscore the label image.
The building codes and regulations for massive and for lightweight walls can sometimes determine the design. The larger the construction project, the greater the requirements for fire- and sound protection. The same is true for guidelines with regard to dividing walls between individual units.

The material selection is even greater for wall panelling as the requirements for a wall covering are fairly low. Panelling can fulfill a variety of functions in the context of the design concept:
• integrate the lighting concept,
• meet the acoustic requirements,
• serve as a media installation surface,
• reveal or hide installations.

To achieve the lead equivalent required to meet radiation protection standards, the exterior of the gypsum board x-ray cabin in the orthodontic practice in Ramstein (shown in fig. 3.4) was sheathed in a visible cladding of sheet lead. This detail also signals the function of the room. Beech strips hide the joints between the sheets and protect the soft lead cladding against mechanical damage. Wall panelling can be attached in two ways. Aside from invisible fastening methods such as suspension systems, mounting strips, adhesives or hidden fasteners, such as fasteners set into joints, there are a variety of visible clip-on systems whose theme it is to make the fasteners (screws, notches, rivets) visible. There are also flush screw mountings and

3.7

3.8

other options, all of which must always be adapted to the material and the structural requirements.

Ceilings
Function: spatial enclosure, roof, covering, load-bearing/non-loadbearing, screening (sound, light, safety, radiation), transparent/translucent, installation carrier, facework, lining, ceiling with built-in components (fire-, sound protection etc.), lighting carrier, light deflection, heating, cooling, air conditioning, and zoning.

Existing Ceilings
Once again the process must begin with an analysis of the existing building substance. The renewal requirements for ceilings, which are integrated into the design, are more or less the same as those planners have to take into consideration for walls, although structural concerns are especially important in the case of ceilings. The location of beams, old panelling and stucco as well as historic floor coverings frequently make it difficult and expensive to open ceilings for the purpose of analysis.

New Ceilings
The first step in the planning is the design dependent differentiation between massive and suspended ceilings. When the shell construction is being designed at the same time, the architect can influence the execution of the load-bearing, massive ceilings (floor slabs and roofs). He can integrate ceiling penetrations and openings for lighting, installations or access into his design. The ceilings can be designed to expose the construction, that is bare, or with a top finish. Suspended substructures can be used to hide installations. Systems ceilings with metal, gypsum, glass, fibre board or wood panels facilitate access to installations for maintenance or modification. These solutions also facilitate the integration of technical characteristics such as cooling, heating, light deflection, lighting and ventilation.
Continuous ceilings, composed of taped gypsum panels, for example, make it possible to install ceilings mirrors without joints. It is important, however, to plan in advance where maintenance openings and light and ventilation slits are going to be located, since access to the cavity above system ceilings is limited. Ceiling joints and transitions to other building materials should be carefully executed to avoid undesired shadows and reflections. Whenever the design allows for shadow joints, this approach offers a clean separation of the ceiling from other building components and also the inconspicuous installation of intake- and exhaust air vents. Gypsum board ceilings can, with simple measures, easily meet all the necessary requirements with regard to fire protection and acoustics (or sound insulation). Unless there are other structural demands on the ceilings, the selection of available materials is wide-ranging: expanded metal, glass, wood, textiles etc. offer considerable freedom in design. Thus the suspended ceiling sails in the Bayerischen Kunstgewerbeverein in Munich (fig. 3.9) divide the plan into zones and structure the image of the space. They establish a geometric relationship to the individual functional areas of the plan and simultaneously integrate the lighting concept. The gypsum board elements were prefabricated off-site, guaranteeing precision in the edging; threaded rods were used for the suspension. The fluorescent tubes for indirect

lighting are housed directly behind the gypsum board edges, the adjustable downlights, which accentuate individual areas, were cut into the panels after installation.

Stairs

The visual integration of a staircase into the overall concept for an interior design with regards to the geometry of the plan, material selection, transitions to adjacent building components and lighting (natural or artificial light) is of tremendous importance. The spatial construct can be deliberately continued or interrupted by designing a solid staircase or a lighter, more filigree staircase. Interior staircase can be purely functional or creatively designed three-dimensional sculptures, although the latter too must meet established standards and guidelines. The technical and official guidelines for staircase construction have been extensively documented. Depending on the personal safety requirements of the users, exemptions may be authorized by the client and allow the planner to implement customized solutions that do not reflect standard guidelines. Linking the strings and treads of staircases to walls are particularly challenging aspects both in terms of construction and design with regard to structural integrity and footfall sound insulation. Additional functions mean that stairs are more than a simple connection of two levels. The stairs shown in figures 3.10 and 3.11 in a four-storey housing complex in Dachau link two apartments, one above the other. The filigree construction penetrates the existing reinforced concrete floor. It is set into the plan as a free sculpture and is transformed into a focal point of the interiors. Two courses of the stairs are freely suspended with the load being transferred via steel blades

3.9

in the risers onto a steel substructure hidden behind the wood panelling. The loads on the landings and the third course are also transferred to the same steel substructure via step-shaped beams. This effectively liberates the stairs from the existing dividing wall between the apartments, avoiding sound transfer between neighbouring units. The banister, which is barely perceptible from the room, consists of toughened safety glass (10 mm) and is integrated into a groove in the steps. The three bonded glass panes of the banister result in the necessary bracing. The wood folds are illuminated by up- and downlights integrated into floor and ceiling, emphasizing the sculptural effect of the staircase.

Furnishings

Interiors can be furnished with series-manufactured pieces, systems that can be completed and expanded, or else by designing and building individual customized pieces. Furniture design offers the advantage of creating the pieces with the appropriate materials and textures to meet the user's specific ideas. In this scenario, the piece of furniture is an integral part of the interior design concept: for example, such pieces can serve as room dividers as in the jewellery boutique in Munich, which will be discussed below. Additional technical functions (lighting, house- and information technology) can also be integrated with precision.

From classic wood carpentry (massive, laminated or untreated) to glass- and steel constructions, concrete- and masonry, synthetics and recycled materials, the choices offer an abundance of design options. Aside from the multitude of materials and combinations, surface treatment also offers a

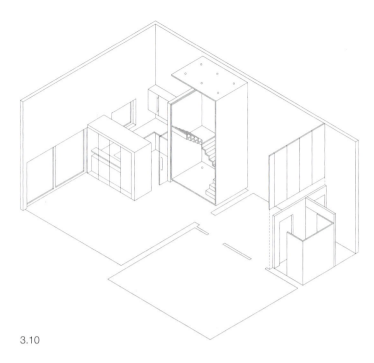

3.10

3.11

wide spectrum of design options. Classic finishes such as lacquers and glazes are complemented by other options such as sandblasting, polishing, brushing, etching and patinating to name but a few. On untreated surfaces, the traces of use (patina) can create a special effect. Natural materials can also change with age and exposure to light – as can surface finishes – thereby changing the appearance of the furniture.

The central room divider in the gallery for contemporary jewellery illustrated on pages 80ff. can serve as an example of how customized furniture can satisfy a variety of demands and unify many different uses in a single piece. The piece divides the gallery into a retail and a workshop area and also serves as an elegant backdrop for the boutique. On the boutique side, the brushed stainless steel divider houses a retractable counter cube, the cashier and showcases. The rear side is finished with a smooth, bleached maple panelled wall divided into compartments in different sizes. The office functions of the gallery are integrated into this side: with a few simple adjustments, the room divider can be transformed into a complete workstation. There is a fold-down desk, additional compartments provide storage space for file folders – even a refrigerator and espresso machine are built-in. The row of display cases visible in the boutique are accessible from this side via simple folding doors. The flush execution of all the details, the invisible magnet fixtures that make handles and other accessories unnecessary contribute to the sculptural effect of this piece. Stainless sheets were mounted onto the board with a veneering press and mixed adhesive and then mitred to achieve precision edges and corners. In addition to selecting the material, the construction of the elements is another important factor that must be considered when designing furniture and built-in furnishings. These considerations determine the dimensions of the panels, their weight and ease of assembly. Transportation to and within the building as well as on-site installation should also be taken into consideration. Construction joints can be executed deliberately visible as shadow joints if they are intended as design tools, or more or less invisible if this is not the case. The individual mounting steps must be integrated into the overall construction plan and co-ordinated with other trades. The planner must consider the frequency of use, the degree and type of stress, durability as well as maintenance and upkeep before selecting materials, fittings (fixed and removable junctions) and surfaces.

Light

Light is an essential component of interior design: lighting influences the effect of materials and their surfaces. It can divide rooms into different zones and illuminate areas according to specific requirements. The atmosphere in a room is defined by the effect of the surfaces in terms of degree of reflection and light density. The colour of the light is an important factor with regard to user comfort and the effect of the illuminated objects. Daylight is the most important type of light in a room; it establishes a link to the outside, although it is important to prevent glare.
Daylight can be directed into the depth of a room via the facades and windows with the help of light deflection systems. The necessary shading and glare protection systems define the design at the interface between interior and

3.12

3.13

exterior. A carefully planned lighting strategy can achieve a link between the interior and exterior space. The effectiveness of shop window areas is dependent on the relationship of the interior lighting to the intensity of the daylight. Thus the blue light of the fluorescent tubes in the cosmetics store in New York (see pages 84ff.) translates into a mysterious glow when seen from the street perspective, literally drawing passers-by into the store.

Artificial light is used as a complement to or replacement for natural light, depending on the use of a particular space. Targeted lighting can be an effective tool for staging building components, display objects or goods (fig. 3.15, 3.16). Light cones, cast shadows, different degrees of brightness and colours are all elements of light planning.

In the bank branch in Munich (fig. 3.14), which has the ambience of a public arcade, the bands of integrated ceiling lights heighten the sense of depth and direction; they also contribute to the visibility of the interior from the Marienplatz, which lies out front. The indirect lighting can be complemented by spotlights mounted on a hidden track.

A double row of ceiling fixtures, equipped with compact fluorescent tubes, provide the 500–750 lux required for monitor workstations. Light simulation scenarios and corresponding calculations carried out by expert planners support the realization of lighting concepts and ensure the required luminous intensity for each area. The user or observer position is the most decisive factor when it comes to locating light sources in a room. It is therefore vital to avoid direct glare from light sources or indirect glare from mirror effects and reflection.

There is a wide variety of lighting units (or luminaires) available for selection depending on the specific spatial situation direct and indirect luminaires, deflecting and reflecting systems, integrated and surface mounted units. Correspondingly, there are many different types of lamps: incandescent lamps for everyday use, high voltage and low voltage halogen lamps, compact- and fluorescent lamps, discharge and special lamps and LED-lamps. With the wide range of lamps available on the market today – from exterior to floor and ceiling lamps, table and floor lamps, floodlights, light deflecting systems and downlights to wall lamps – almost any design task can be realized. This selection is moreover complemented by the option of customized lamps. Aspects such as the thermal output of illuminants must also be taken into consideration from the outset. The radiated heat must be ventilated if necessary to avoid any negative impact on the internal climate and the lit objects. Halogen-metal oxide vaporized mirrors were chosen, for example, to light the display cases in the room divider of the jewellery gallery shown on page 80ff. They deliver the desired brightness and the reflections that emphasize the effect of the pieces on display. The same lighting was also chosen for the stainless steel display cases in the centre of the gallery; here, ventilating the radiated heat was an important consideration.

Lighting for Workstations
When there are great differences in how the workstation and the surrounding areas are illuminated, the constant adjustments the eye is forced to undergo result in fatigue that can lead to long-term visual impairment. It is therefore important to minimize differences in light intensity or luminance. Monitor workstations must also be glare-free.

3.17

dealing with regulatory requirements from building authorities. Public clients or planning departments in large companies naturally complicate the decision-making process; moreover, the transparent, public process of tendering also increases the risk that the desired quality in the execution may not be achieved if the contractors have inadequate experience. The design should therefore take these parameters into consideration. While working with public clients calls for vigilance with regard to the more elaborate organization and co-ordination of the project planning, there is yet another aspect that comes into play with large firms or corporations: interiors for these clients often demand that the corporate design or corporate identity be integrated. This means that specified colours, materials and lettering, shop- and display systems or even standardized furniture systems must be used, and they frequently determine much of the design. Developing a new corporate identity is a unique challenge, since it requires collaboration with graphic designers and advertising agencies, going far beyond the standard range of interior design. New trends and changing client demands continue to confront planners with ever-new challenges in this field.

Current Trends

As in all design fields, there is a multitude of concurrent styles that are being developed for interiors. In this field especially, the sheer number and variety of building tasks, tight schedules for planning and execution and simple options for construction in repeated renovations make it possible to quickly implement the latest trends in architecture. No other field can boast a comparable number of innovative concepts where experimentation with styles leads to ever-new variations of spatial expression. At this point in time they range from pure material minimalism, where reduced form and bare surfaces transform interiors into *objects d'art*, to formal fragments that date back to the 1970s and Pop Art. In addition, many contemporary interiors also contain design elements from the 1920s, 1950s and 1960s – in other words, what we see today is the full range of interior finishing and interior design that evolved over the past decades. Clients who contract architects for retail interiors place especial value on "contemporary" concepts in this sense as a means to promote sales. For this reason, the interior design of retail stores is often the best indicator of current trends. Not all contemporary design concepts for interiors are inspired by looking to past models; innovations in materials and in multi-media also influence the design. New technologies change the behaviour of the users of a room – and the spatial organisation and structure must be adapted to these changes. Moreover, the increased interest in experimenting with new materials has opened new doors for planners, who can work with designs and concepts whose translation can lead to unusual and inspiring interiors.

Illustrations:
3.1 Herz-Jesu-Kirche, Munich, Allmann Sattler Wappner 2000
3.2 Dentist office, Wiesbaden, situation prior to renovation
3.3 Dentist office, Wiesbaden, Landau + Kindelbacher 1997
3.4 Orthodontic practice, Ramstein, Landau + Kindelbacher 1997
3.5 Fashion boutique in New York, Choi-Campagna Design 2000, section
3.6 Fashion boutique in New York, Choi-Campagna Design 2000
3.7 Plaza in Commerzbank headquarters, Frankfurt/Main,
    Alfredo Arribas 1997
3.8 Restoration of an industrial hall, Munich, Thomas Herzog and
    José-Luis Moro 1997, ceiling design
3.9 Bayerischer Kunstgewerbeverein München,
    Landau + Kindelbacher 2000
3.10 Residential conversion, Dachau, Landau + Kindelbacher 1996
    axonometric view
3.11 Residential conversion, Dachau, Landau + Kindelbacher 1996
3.12 Jewellery boutique in Munich, Landau + Kindelbacher 1997,
    central room divider, see also pp. 80ff.
3.13 Jewellery boutique in Munich, Landau + Kindelbacher 1997,
    central room divider, see also pp. 80ff.
3.14 HypoVereinsbank on Marienplatz, Munich,
    Landau + Kindelbacher 2000
3.15 Waterloo Station, London, Nicholas Grimshaw & Partners 1993,
    detail of ceiling light
3.16 Waterloo Station, London, Nicholas Grimshaw & Partners 1993
3.17 Sports centre, Davos, Gigon/Guyer 1996
3.18 Prada Store, New York, OMA/AMO 2001

3.18

The Examples

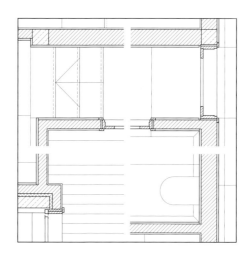 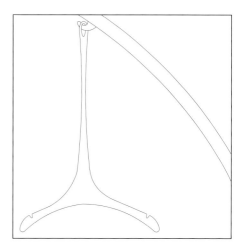

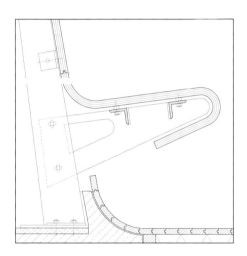 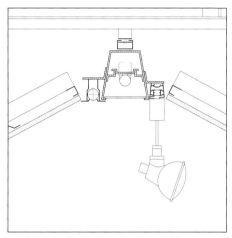 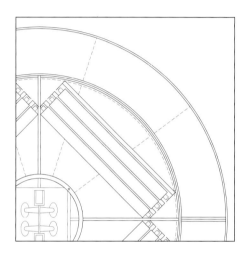

Dining and catering spaces

Spaces for work

Arts and cultural spaces

Transport spaces

House in Vila Nova de Famalicão

Architect: Alvaro Siza Vieira, Porto

The brief required the erection of a villa on the stone founda-
tions of an unfinished earlier structure, as well as the rehabilita-
tion of a smaller house and the landscaping of the grounds.
Situated on the southern slopes of Monte St Catarina north of
the industrial city of Famalicão in Portugal, the site has an area
of 20,000 m² and is terraced with stone walls. The fine stock of
old oak and pine trees is echoed by the oak finishings of the
interior design. The interplay between the many offset planes
of the building and the visual links that are established is
reflected internally in the spatial organization of the villa.
The entrance is unobtrusively located in a single-storey tract
that also houses the ancillary rooms. On advancing into the
foyer, the internal space unfolds into a two-storey vestibule
flooded with light. From here, a ramp leads down into a flowing
sequence of spaces, including the dining room, living room
and lounge areas, which afford a wealth of visual links and
views out to the surrounding landscape.
The fitting out and finishings are based largely on the effect of
wood and the sparse use of furnishings, to which the white
plastered wall surfaces form a restrained background. The
layout of the open living area, which is focused on the fireplace, enhances the generous sense of space. The eye of the
visitor is drawn upwards to the roof lights. From here, daylight
flows down the white plastered walls to illuminate the ground
floor spaces. The uniform oak flooring in the living areas harmonizes with the wall linings and in-built fittings in the same
material. In the kitchen and bathrooms, the floors and walls are
finished with sand-coloured marble, which is contrasted with
the wood window frames and furnishings.

Section
Floor plans
scale 1:400

 1 Entrance
 2 Garage
 3 Foyer
 4 Laundry room
 5 Utilities room
 6 Bathroom/WC/
   Dressing room
 7 Kitchen
 8 Dining room
 9 Living room
10 Bedroom
11 Terrace/Balcony
12 Void
13 Roof light

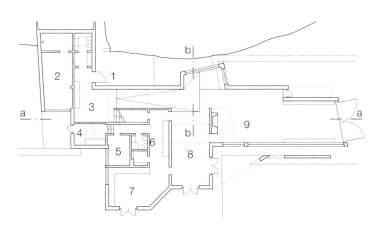

46

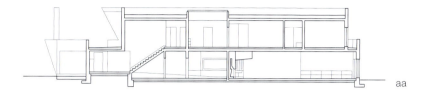

aa

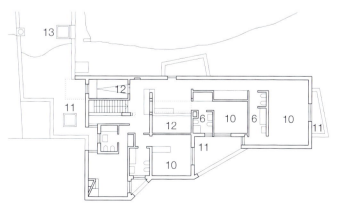

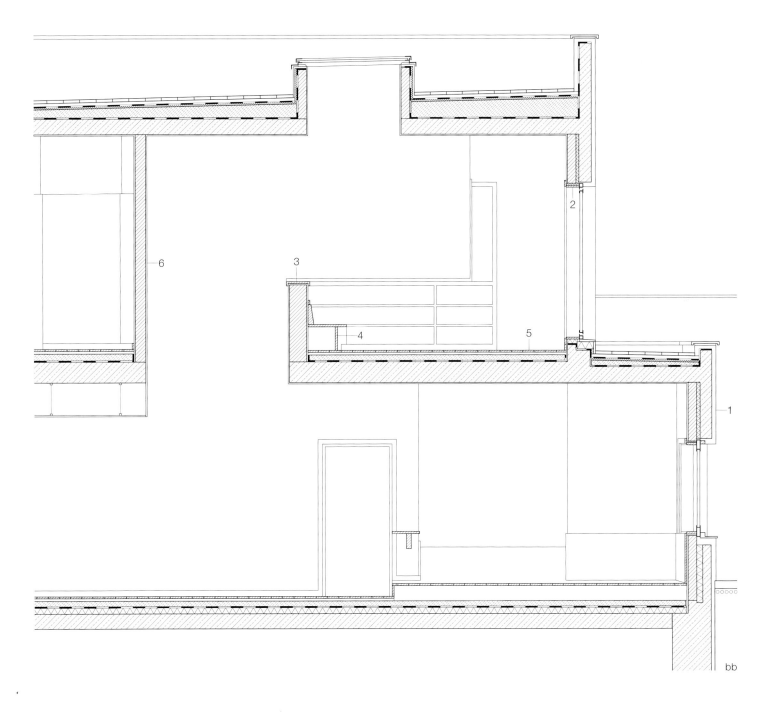

1 wall construction:
   70 mm insulating
   rendering
   150 mm reinforced
   concrete skin
   40 mm core insulation
   115 mm brick skin
   15 mm plaster

2 35 mm oak lining
   to reveal
3 30 mm oak top
   to parapet wall
4 35 mm oak bench
5 gallery floor construction:
   25 mm oak boarding
   40 mm battens

   80 mm screed
   separating layer
   250 mm reinforced
   concrete floor slab
   15 mm plaster
6 115 mm brick wall
   with 15 mm plaster
   on both faces

Horizontal sections
scale 1:50

1 wall construction:
  70 mm insulating rendering
  150 mm reinforced
  concrete skin
  40 mm core insulation
  115 mm brick skin
  15 mm plaster

2 25 mm Lioz marble
  wall lining
  115 mm brick wall
  15 mm plaster
3 35 mm oak lining to reveal
4 15 mm plaster
  200 mm brickwork
5 25 mm Lioz marble
  wall lining
  115 mm brickwork

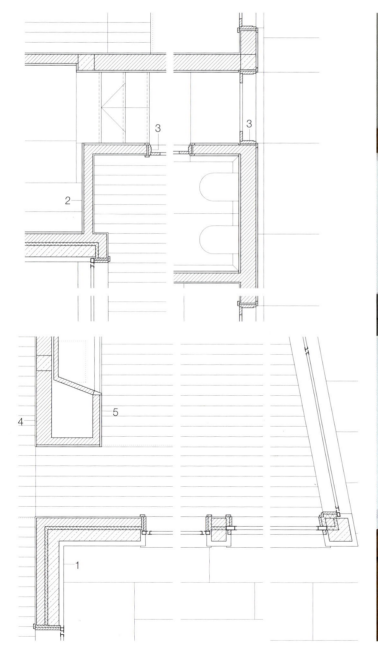

Attic in Vienna

Architects: Hubmann & Vass, Vienna

This newly built attic provides additional space for a two-storey house. Its 230 m² of living space are distributed along a continuous, narrow corridor, forming a private and a communal area. Built-in plywood units are used as furniture or structured like furniture, and thus define the space in this development. The load-bearing structure is built into the chimney wall, so that it does not impinge on the living area. It can be discerned in the position of the windows, which extend along the full length of the dwelling as roof-lights and side glazing. Two box fixtures placed in the living-space face the 24 m long continuous band of windows. These contain the kitchen and the bathroom, and at the same time structure the large leisure area. They can be made into enclosed spaces by means of sliding doors.

These boxes, like all the fitted elements and the numerous sliding doors are clad in plywood with three coats of paint, and the entire attic floor – except in the bathroom – is in oak parquet. The worktops and wet areas in the two boxes are covered with intricate grey mosaic tiles, with contrasting flat wall elements in exposed concrete. The use of a reinforced concrete load-bearing structure with continuous steel purlins meant that the entire ridge area could be glazed, with the exception of the existing chimneys. The continuous windows running the length of the attic and the generous opening on to the roof terrace make for an interior that positively revels in light.

The reduced number of materials and restrained colour scheme create a peaceful framework for the fluent spatial continuum, which can be constantly transformed by means of the many sliding elements.

Axonometric diagram
large-scale timber fittings
Section · plan 1:250

1 Entrance	6 Living
2 Corridor	7 Working
3 Kitchen	8 Dining area
4 Bathroom	9 Bedroom
5 WC	10 Terrace

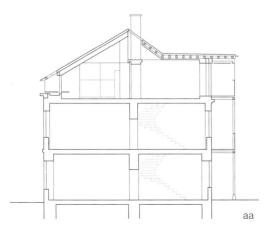

aa

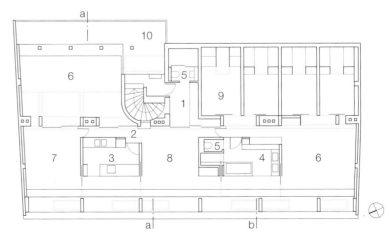

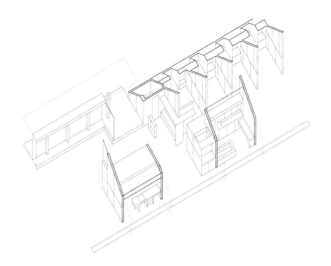

Section · Bathroom ground plan   scale 1:20

1 2 layers of tiles
   30 + 50 mm layers of battens
   roofing felt
   24 mm boarding ventilated
   180 mm heat insulation
   vapour barrier
   2× 12.5 mm plasterboard
2 5 + 12 + 5 mm double glazing
3 38 mm veneered plywood bench
4 veneered plywood sliding door
5 22 mm oak parquet on screed
6 mosaic tiles on screed
7 22 mm veneered plywood
8 built-in lamp
9 glazing 8 mm toughened
   safety glass

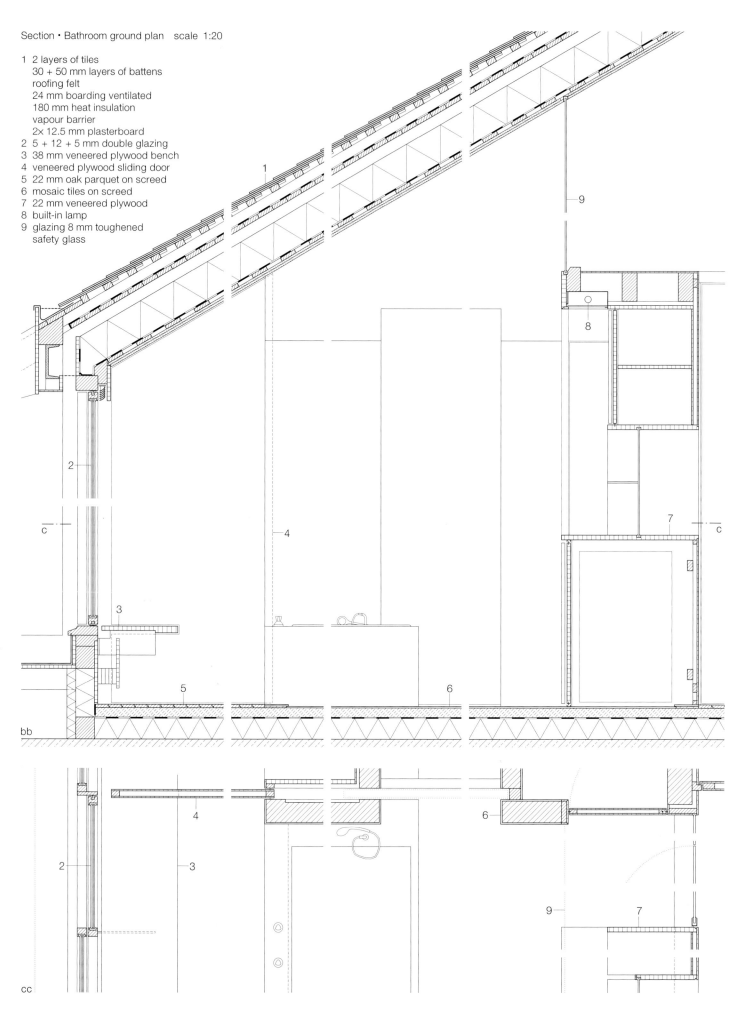

Duplex Apartment in New York

Architects: Maya Lin in collaboration with David Hotson, New York

Located in the centre of New York, this apartment is designed to accommodate four people. The two floor levels are offset to the street by half a storey in height, with the large living-dining area situated below street level. A maximum exploitation of the limited amount of daylight that enters the dwelling was a central consideration of the design, therefore, as the bright, friendly character of the rooms indicates.

The internal space is articulated by an almost graphic interplay between wall planes and lighting accents. All structural measures and inbuilt elements were reduced to a minimum to enhance this effect. An example of this is the staircase that separates the living room from the kitchen. This central, space-defining element plays a special role in the design. The upper landing, the two flights of stairs and the intermediate landing – which affords access to all areas of the apartment – are supported by a vertical steel plate braced by steel bars welded on to the surface and sunk into the timber construction. The dividing wall between the two stair flights rises freely through the dwelling. On the side facing the living room, it is clad in maple; on the kitchen face, it is in exposed steel.

The top landing is also detached from the two-storey, etched, rear-lighted glass wall, which extends over the full height of the space, creating a visual link between the two levels of the apartment. For the larger of the two bedrooms, the architects designed pivoting cupboard and door elements, which allow the room to be divided. The outcome is an evocative spatial composition in which daylight flows round the various discrete elements, thereby demonstrating their structural independence as well as revealing the different qualities of the materials.

Section · Floor plans
scale 1:250

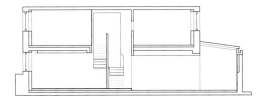

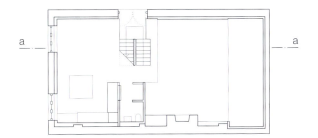

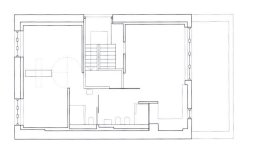

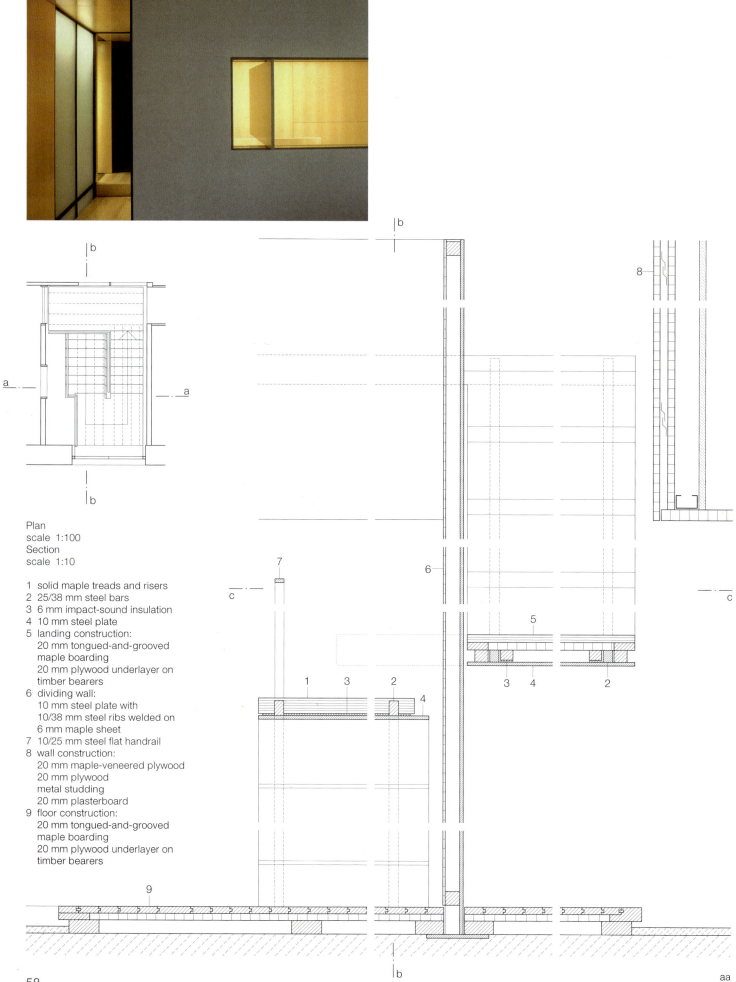

Plan
scale 1:100
Section
scale 1:10

1 solid maple treads and risers
2 25/38 mm steel bars
3 6 mm impact-sound insulation
4 10 mm steel plate
5 landing construction:
   20 mm tongued-and-grooved
   maple boarding
   20 mm plywood underlayer on
   timber bearers
6 dividing wall:
   10 mm steel plate with
   10/38 mm steel ribs welded on
   6 mm maple sheet
7 10/25 mm steel flat handrail
8 wall construction:
   20 mm maple-veneered plywood
   20 mm plywood
   metal studding
   20 mm plasterboard
9 floor construction:
   20 mm tongued-and-grooved
   maple boarding
   20 mm plywood underlayer on
   timber bearers

aa

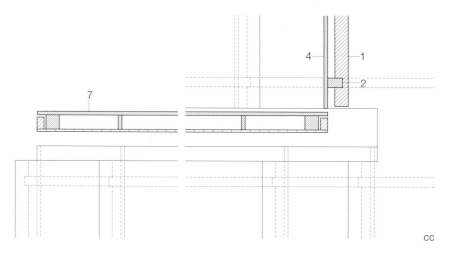

4 ─ 1

2

7

cc

Sections   scale 1:10

1 solid maple treads and risers
2 25/38 mm steel bars
3 6 mm impact-sound insulation
4 10 mm welded steel plate
5 landing and gallery construction:
   20 mm tongued-and-grooved
   maple boarding
   20 mm plywood underlayer on
   timber bearers

6 steel door (1/2 hr. fire resistance)
   with maple-veneer finish
7 dividing wall:
   10 mm steel plate with 10/38 mm
   steel ribs welded on
   6 mm maple sheet
8 20 mm plasterboard on 20 mm plywood
9 balustrade construction:
   10 mm steel plate
   intermediate layer
   20 mm maple-veneered plywood

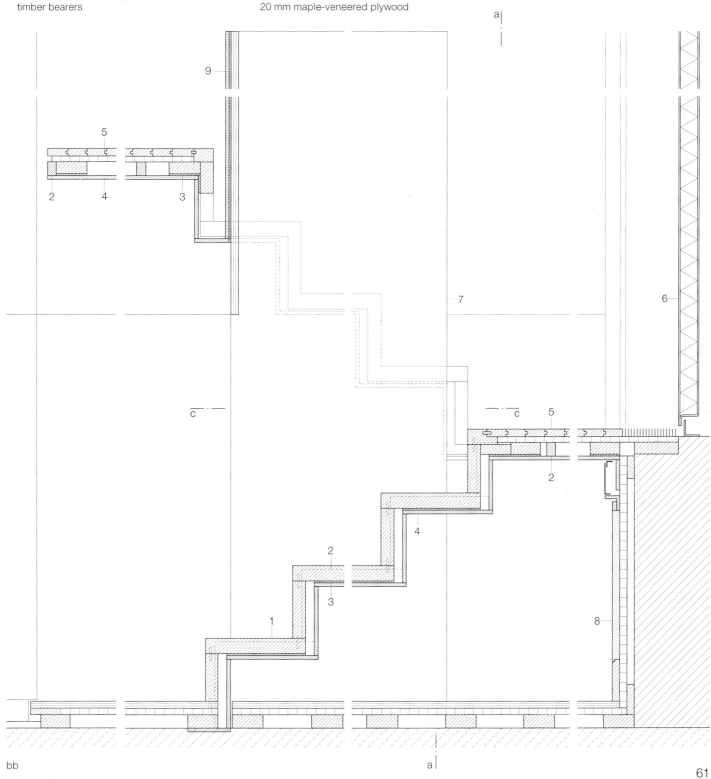

bb

House in Ito

Architects: Motoyoshi Itagaki & Hiromi Sugimoto, Tokyo

A small, specially planted bamboo garden appears when the sliding doors to the two large, traditionally designed living areas are open. It conveys a sense of peace and isolation in the middle of a densely built-up area. The house – planned as a refuge for the winter months - does not cover a very large area, but it is three storeys high and is furnished in the style of a Japanese home. The reinforced concrete ground floor also serves as a retaining wall in the downward-sloping terrain, and the two upper storeys, which contain the actual living accommodation, are timber-built. On the ground floor, next to the two living areas, there is also a small room for the tea ceremony. Light "yuki-mishoji" sliding screens are used to divide the rooms, rather than fixed intermediate walls. Even when they are closed they give an enhanced sense of spatial continuity and experience. The miniature garden becomes part of the interior: an image of meditative landscape for occupants seeking peace and quiet.

The window shown in detail consists of several sliding elements: a wooden shutter to keep out the wind and rain, an insect-proof screen, a glazed section and an interior sliding paper screen to modulate the light. The construction points up the idea of the fluid ground plan linking inside and outside: there is no definite open or shut state, just finely graded ways of modulating the exterior for the interior – the sensitivity of Japanese spatial awareness is expressed in the system of sliding elements.

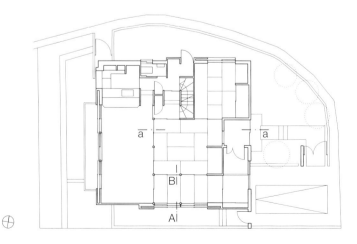

Ground floor plan
scale 1:250

The living areas in the traditional Japanese style all have characteristically lucid articulation, and spatial links that also include the garden. Individual rooms can be partitioned off by sliding elements when necessary, to provide private spaces. The room sizes are strictly based on the dimensions of the Tatami mats.

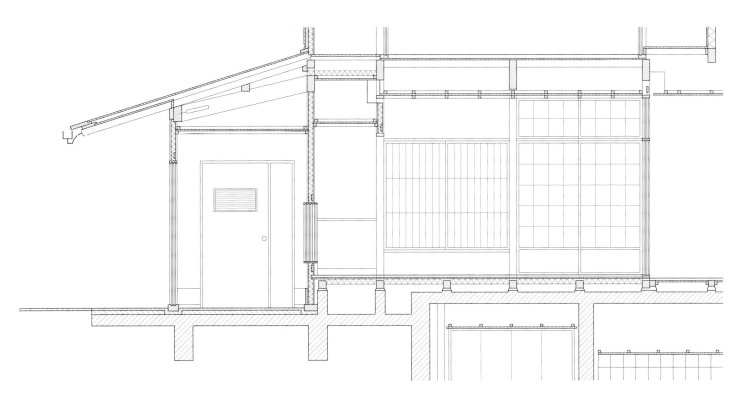

section
scale 1:50

A Window detail
B Sliding wall detail
 Vertical and horizontal sections
 scale 1:10

Sliding elements:
wood frame
with
1 plywood panels
2 insect screen
3 glass
4 paper

5 sheet copper
 covering
6 hardwood inlay
7 tatami mat
8 wall recess for wood
 sliding shutter
9 110/110 mm timber column

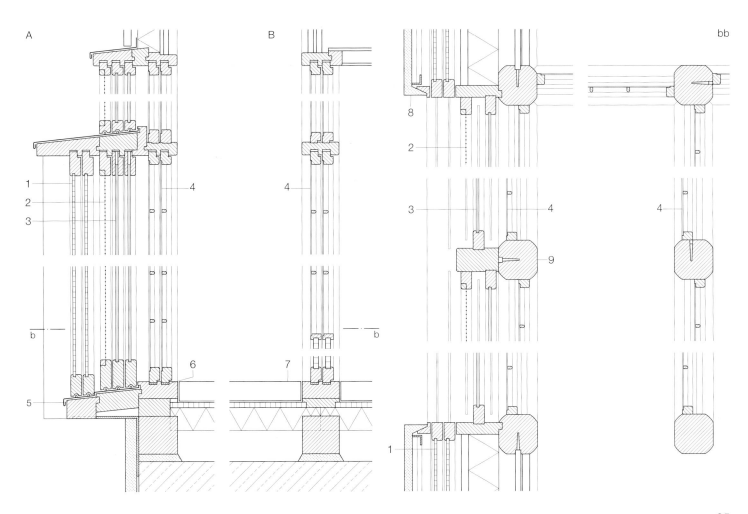

Chapel in Valleacerón

Architects: Sancho Madridejos, Madrid

The sky with its rushing dark clouds and the barren, rocky landscape make a perfect frame for this place of worship in Castille-La Mancha, the Spanish region in which Don Quixote tilted against windmills. The chapel has exposed concrete surfaces inside and outside. It stands on a little eminence, itself like one of the scattered rocks: the rough surfaces of the materials correspond with the barren surroundings.

The exposed site on a little hill makes the building into a fixed point of the kind used by surveyors. It is based on a set of studies, and its sculptural looking cubatures developed from these into a folded cube. The tilting and folding walls of the cuboid create a tension-filled volume that visitors come into through a narrow gap in the west facade.

Inside the walls are staggered in relation to each other, thus creating different spatial impressions. Although the ground plan suggests a single space, the proportions of that space change according to the viewpoint and the light penetrating into the interior through the apertures in the building formed by the staggering of the wall surfaces. Visitors have the feeling of moving through a sequence of spaces – closed, tight, open or fragmented – complemented by views out into the countryside at specific points. The relationship between inside and outside determines the different spatial impressions. There are no distracting additional furnishings here, no artificial lighting, the space can speak entirely for itself. Only a simple cross on the east facade indicates what the building is for. The glazing in the apertures continues the folding principle and is articulated by steel glazing bars. The entrance doorway is cut into one of these glass surfaces in the form of a box. Here too the folding principle is followed through consistently.

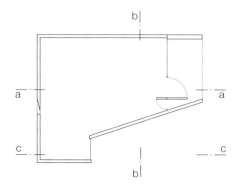

Plan
Sections
scale 1:250

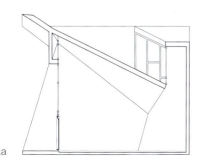

aa

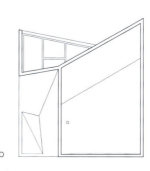

bb

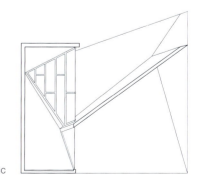

cc

section
scale 1:20

1 Sealing plastic coating
2 200 mm reinforced concrete
3 Galvanized steel sheet
  painted in concrete colour
4 laminated safety glass 2x 8 mm
5 I beam 200 mm deep
6 Entrance door
  frame 300 mm steel RHS
  door leaf hollow 2x 2.5 mm sheet steel
7 Floor polished reinforced concrete
window bars, steel girders and door
oxidized on site, matt painted

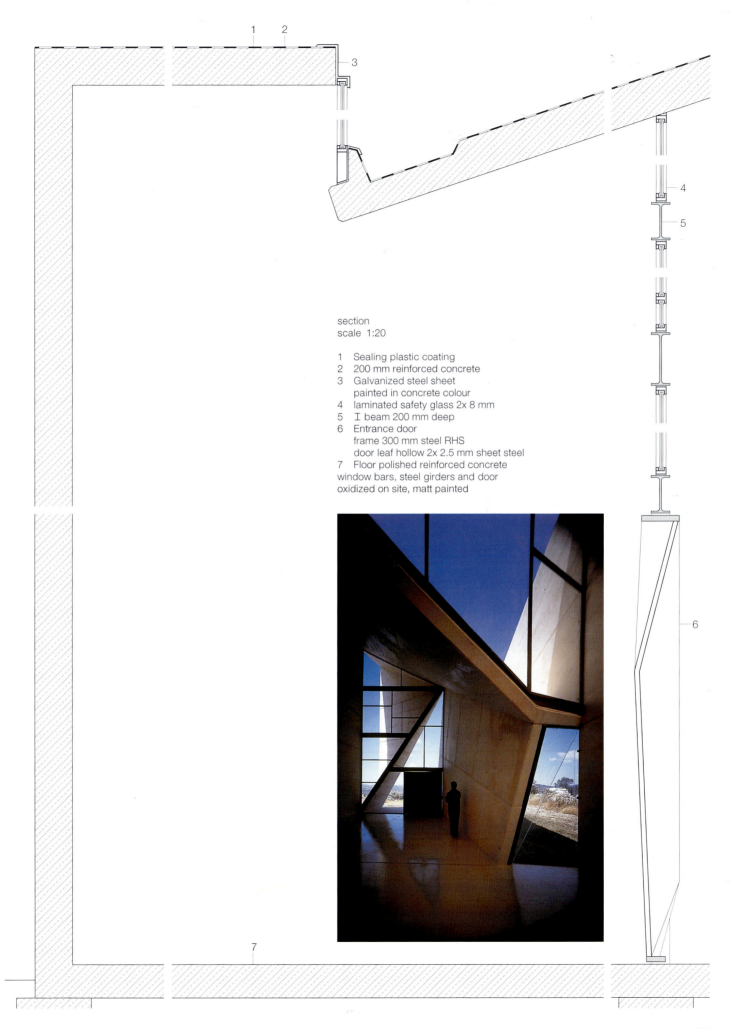

69

Synagogue in Dresden

Architects: Wandel Hoefer Lorch + Hirsch, Saarbrücken

The site that used to be occupied by the old synagogue is at the end of the Brühl Terraces, in the immediate vicinity of the Zwinger in Dresden. The new building has two sections, which provide a sense of articulation for the long plot: between the community centre and the synagogue proper is a courtyard with a grove of plane trees and rough waste glass rammed into sand, which follows the ground plan of the old synagogue. Behind this is the windowless cube of the synagogue, twisting upwards like a screw so that the building follows tradition by facing east. A synagogue is both a temple and an ark of the covenant (where the Thora scrolls are kept). The architects interpreted these traditional characteristics in the interior through the contrast between solid masonry and a softly falling fabric of metal threads. The translucent baldacchino is suspended from the concrete ceiling, and its golden shimmer defines the actual central place of worship. A lamp glowing in a warm orange indicates the central lectern and the fact that it faces east. The daylight admitted by the roof-lights is further complemented by other lamps suspended from the ceiling and also by spots built into the side walls. They light the area surrounding the actual place of worship; visitors become aware that it faces east because of the changing geometry. The metal threads of the ark reflect the light and lend a shimmer of unreality to the prayer room and the area around it. The furnishings: the gallery at the west end, seating, alemor (lectern) and Thora shrine at the east end are in brown-stained oak. Their colour contrasts with the light, shimmering character of the metal fabric. They are plain and unadorned, without any superfluous accessories, and thus seem entirely unpretentious. The clear forms of the fittings and their highly crafted quality help to assert the interior's concentrated yet reticent appearance.

Section · Plan
scale 1:1250

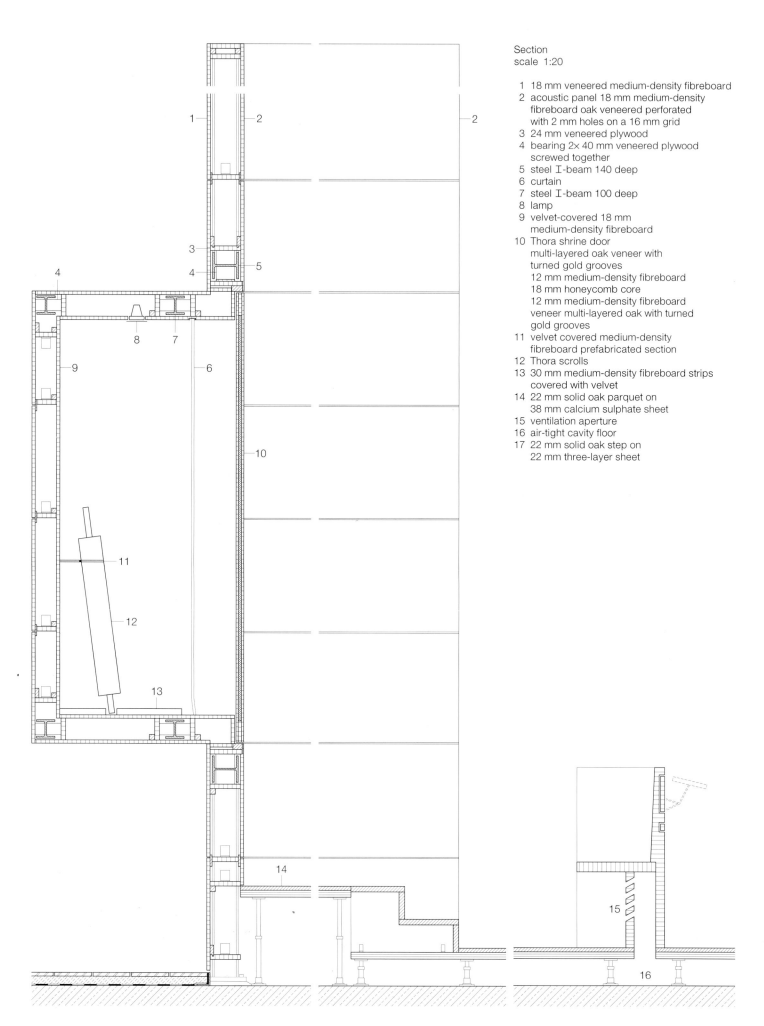

Section
scale 1:20

1 18 mm veneered medium-density fibreboard
2 acoustic panel 18 mm medium-density
   fibreboard oak veneered perforated
   with 2 mm holes on a 16 mm grid
3 24 mm veneered plywood
4 bearing 2× 40 mm veneered plywood
   screwed together
5 steel I-beam 140 deep
6 curtain
7 steel I-beam 100 deep
8 lamp
9 velvet-covered 18 mm
   medium-density fibreboard
10 Thora shrine door
   multi-layered oak veneer with
   turned gold grooves
   12 mm medium-density fibreboard
   18 mm honeycomb core
   12 mm medium-density fibreboard
   veneer multi-layered oak with turned
   gold grooves
11 velvet covered medium-density
   fibreboard prefabricated section
12 Thora scrolls
13 30 mm medium-density fibreboard strips
   covered with velvet
14 22 mm solid oak parquet on
   38 mm calcium sulphate sheet
15 ventilation aperture
16 air-tight cavity floor
17 22 mm solid oak step on
   22 mm three-layer sheet

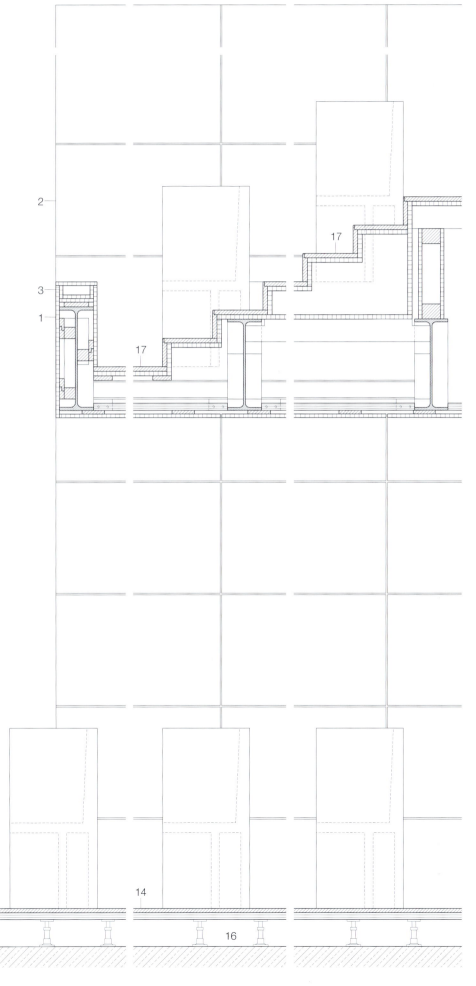

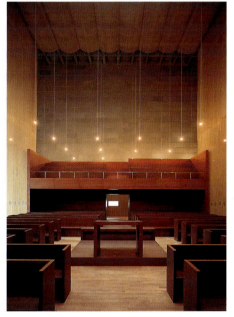

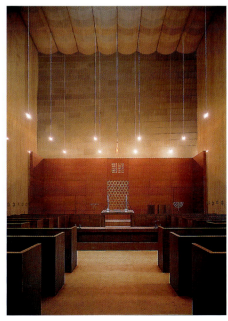

Kindergarten in Lustenau

Architects: Dietrich and Untertrifaller, Bregenz

The spatial requirements of kindergartens are many and varied. A standard brief would call for rooms for physical and creative activities, as well as flexible group rooms that permit a wide range of uses. The architecture, of course, must be designed to meet the needs of children. With their warm surface coloration, the internal spaces of this kindergarten in Lustenau, Austria, radiate a bright, friendly atmosphere and a pleasantly restrained character that afford the children scope for personal development and self-discovery.

The kindergarten consists of two sections: an end structure containing the ancillary spaces and a basement; and a linear tract with south-facing rooms for group activities. The latter is constructed of prefabricated hollow-section elements and opens on to the garden.

The elongated tract has a varied articulation internally. Each of the group rooms is divided into a rear space with a gallery, and a front space roughly 4.20 metres high extending over the full height of the building.

Roof lights ensure an even distribution of daylight. Only the zone beneath the gallery is somewhat darker. Here, children can withdraw from the groups, while still remaining in visual contact with the others.

The front area of the room is suitable for games and activities on a larger scale and can be extended outdoors in the summer months. The furnishings, walls and soffits radiate a uniformly warm tone of wood, which extends over the entire interior in the form of light-coloured birch veneer or plywood cladding. The glass balustrades to the galleries also ensure that the children have an unimpeded view of the garden, which forms a common play area where the individual groups are united in their activities.

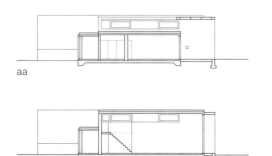

aa

bb

Sections
Floor plan
scale 1:400

1 Entrance
2 Cloakroom
3 Group room
4 Gallery area
5 Rest room
6 Kitchen
7 Spare room
8 Office

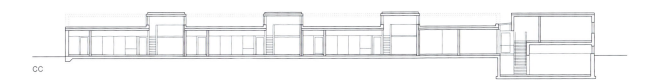

cc

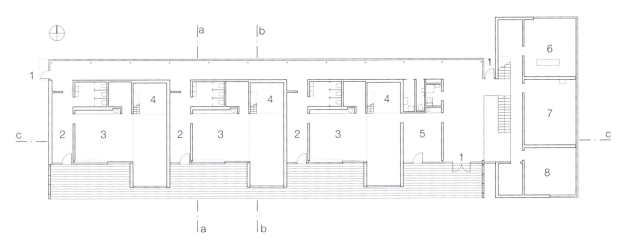

Horizontal section
Vertical section through cupboard
Vertical section through washing recess
scale 1:20

1 19 mm chipboard
   with melamine-resin coating
   and solid birch nosings to edges
   2× 12.5 mm plasterboard
   120 mm metal studding
   and mineral-wool insulation
   2× 12.5 mm plasterboard
2 19 mm birch-veneered chipboard
   with plywood nosings to edges
3 40 mm birch-veneered chipboard

   door with solid birch frame
4 16 mm birch plywood
5 2 mm blockboard cross-bracing
   to plinth with openings for ventilation runs
6 19 mm chipboard plinth
   with melamine-resin coating
   and ventilation slit
7 36 mm chipboard top
   with melamine-resin coating and
   solid birch nosings to edges

Sectional details
scale 1:5

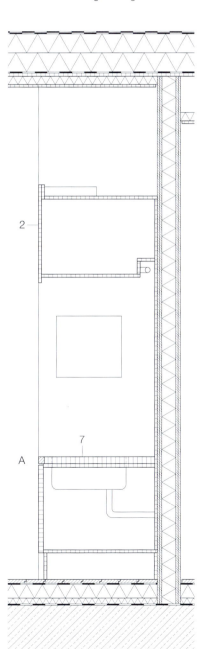

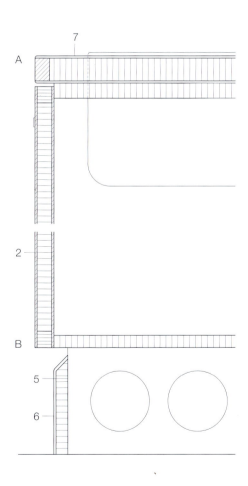

aa   bb

Fashion Boutique in Munich

Architects: Petzinka Pink Architekten, Düsseldorf

This exclusive boutique is one of a series of fashion outlets that the architects have designed in a similar style: simple, lucid volumes create a restrained background appropriate to the image of the goods on sale. The furniture and fittings are largely transparent, providing a discreet framework for presentation, sales and advice.

In the case of this two-storey shop in central Munich, where the newly installed elements simply complement the existing spatial structure, large display windows offer a clear view of the interior. The use of a limited number of materials and uncluttered shapes emphasizes the character of the furnishings: glass, chromium-plated steel or stainless steel, Alpine ash and wenge. The matt shimmer of the glass contrasts with the warm colours of the wood and the light-coloured floor-covering (polished artificial stone slabs on the ground floor, sisal on the top floor).

The till block is on the ground floor, and completely clad with panes of etched glass on the saleroom side, so that customers cannot see the equipment built into it. This fixture is in keeping with the banisters of the staircase behind it leading to the top floor. The shelving system is assembled from tubular steel, and clothes rails can be added as needed; the glazed sections are secured between the stainless steel frames or fastened directly to the wall on tracks. Showcases and display tables are in clear glass with veneered derived timber boards. Floor-to-ceiling mirrors leaning on the walls create an interplay of movement and space – it is not just the exclusive clothes that are on display, the customers are too.

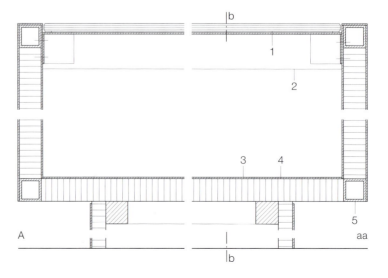

A Longitudinal section display table   scale 1:5
B Cross-section display table   scale 1:5
C Cross section till counter   scale 1:5

 1 10 mm clear glass top
 2 50/50/2 mm stainless steel channel section
 3 2 mm matt chrome sheet brass
 4 30 mm plywood sheeting
 5 30/30 mm stainless steel SHS
 6 fluorescent tube
 7 10 mm toughened glass with etched outer face
 8 slot for till receipt
 9 till printer compartment, slides out
10 pressboard painted on the glass side
11 plywood sheeting
     surfaces veneered in wenge
12 cable runs
13 15/15/2 mm aluminium angle
14 50/50/5 mm stainless steel angle

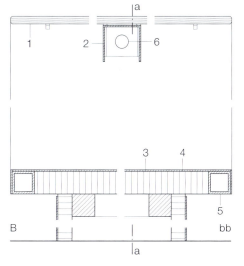

Jewellery Boutique in Munich

Architects: Landau + Kindelbacher, Munich

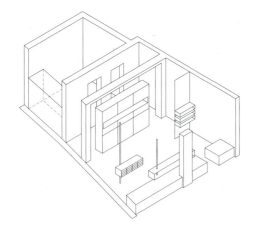

This little shop, which was converted for use as a jewellery boutique with attached workshop, is near the centre of Munich. Visitors can look into the discreetly furnished sales area from the street. The internal divisions were fixed by the existing building; the wall between the workshop and the sales area was largely removed, and fittings were mounted the remaining sections. The architectural design was intended to reflect the prestigious nature of the jewellery, and then to draw attention to the exhibits that are on sale. The sales area serves as a neutral envelope for the built-in furniture. The walls and floor were taken back to their rough state and left unclad: the existing mastic asphalt is sealed with a grey coating, the rear wall of the sales area is finished in grey filler. The reduced treatment of the surfaces underlines the exquisite look of the fittings. The jewellery is displayed at eye-level in the showcase in the shop window, which was developed first – the horizontal, long, low format was then adopted for the other showcases. The eye is drawn into the depth of the space by the glazed rear wall, an effect that is further reinforced by the use of the same colour for the floor and the back wall of the shop. Another display element is the maple-veneered wooden cube fastened to a stainless-steel rod. Its 16 drawers can be opened at will, but each drawer can be closed with a pane of glass, to prevent direct access to the items of jewellery. The cube can be turned through 90 degrees, to produce different spatial situations. During the day it faces the sales area, but at night it is swung towards to display window. On the wall to the right of the entrance, three stainless steel showcases placed one above the other thrust out from the wall. They too can be closed at the back by a room-high sliding glass door.

But the defining element is the central room divider with a bar cube that can be slid out on rails – the front is clad in brushed stainless steel, and the back is in the form of a flat panel with bleached maple veneer, concealing storage space for the workshop area: if necessary, a desk can be folded out, and other compartments contain filing space; a fridge and an espresso machine have also been provided. All the folding items fit flush, and magnetic catches ensure a smoothly sculptural finish. This item is divided into three at the front, and has a continuous display area lit by integral spotlights built into it. To ensure a restful view of the ceiling from below, the 50 watt halogen ceiling lights were built into parallel troughs, so that the light-sources are not directly visible. The runner for the glass sliding door is also built into one of the lighting troughs. The carefully crafted fittings have become the hallmark of the gallery.

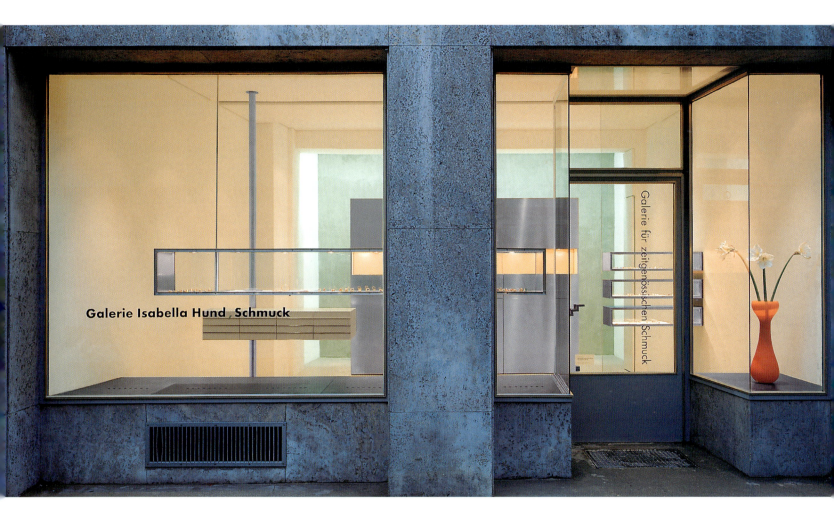

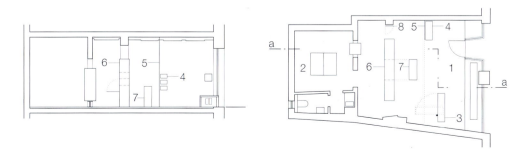

Section · ground floor plan   scale 1:200

1 showroom
2 workshop
3 revolving drawer unit
4 three stainless steel showcases
5 floor-to-ceiling sliding glass screen
   to close off 6
6 room divider with showcases,
   office function from the rear
7 pull-out bar
8 mirror as fold-out panel

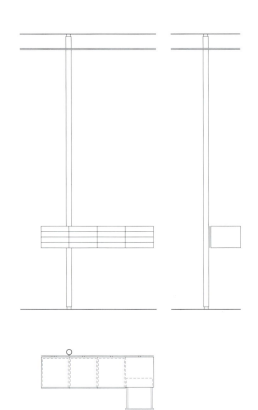

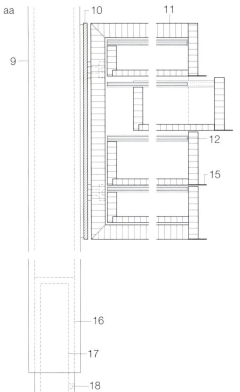

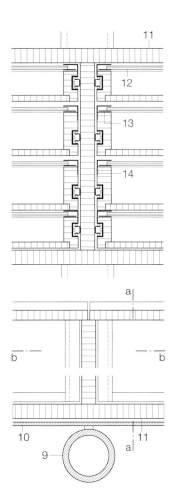

aa

9

10   11
12
15

11
12
13
14

a
b   b
10   11
9   a

16
17
18

Three-part showcase
Elevations · Top view
scale 1:50
Details   scale 1:5

 1 10 mm toughened glass
    sliding door
 2 20/20/2 mm SHS
 3 1.5 mm sheet metal, brush finished
 4 20 watt halogen lamp, flush with soffit
 5 5 mm toughened glass
    adhesive fixed to wood strips
 6 80/80/8 mm steel section,
    fixed in concrete soffit
    with steel head plate
    (side walls too friable)
 7 10 mm steel plate, painted
 8 hexagon-slot screw, countersunk
all metal elements stainless steel except 6

Drawer element
Elevations · Top view   scale 1:50
Details   scale 1:5

 9 70 mm dia. tube 8 mm thick, matt polished
10 5 mm sheet metal back
11 19 mm wood laminboard
    knife-cut veneer in faded maple
12 4 mm glass sheet
    fixed to side of drawes with mortise lock
13 metal sliding strip, adhesive fixed
    to bottom edge of glass
14 19/19 mm metal angle track
    for sliding glass panel
15 1 mm sheet metal grip
16 54 mm dia. metal tube 8 mm thick, welded to 9
17 38 mm brass bott with head plate, fixed to floor
18 grub fixing screw
all metal elements stainless steel

cc

dd

Cosmetics Shop in New York

Architects: Architecture Research Office, New York

The Shiseido cosmetics company's sales outlet and treatment studios are in the best possible location, in the city centre (535 Madison Avenue). The shop is intended for the application and presentation of the new Qiora product range. ARO, a group of young New York architects, have designed it as an open landscape of transparent fabrics, entirely in blue. All the hard edges in the room are hidden behind the translucent strips of material. The carefully judged interplay of materials, shapes and lighting creates a peaceful atmosphere that feels almost unreal; this permeates through the large windows and out into the street, thus enticing people into the shop. The interior décor borrows from the new product range; the curves in the strips of fabric hanging from the ceiling pick up the shapes of the extravagantly designed little flasks and bottles, thus underlining the brand image.

The proportions of the shop, which was specially chosen for its narrow ground plan and great height, correspond with the slender vessels. The products on display are arranged with refined discretion on little tables or on glass shelves on the wall behind transparent curtains. To preserve the fluent, light character of the interior, the service area is placed along the south wall. The area at the back contains individual booths, separated by curved, textile-covered walls and concealed behind the strips of material hanging from the ceiling. The substructure consists of steel girders to which plaster-fibre sheets are attached, also covered in fabric. The lighting is also consistent with the concept of the new product range. All the light sources are concealed, and the indirect lighting underlines the idea of "shining from inside" for which the product stands.

ground floor plan
scale 1:250

1 Retail area
2 Consultation area
3 Spa cabin
4 Lounge
5 Gentlemen's bath
6 Ladies' bath
9 Ladies' dressing area

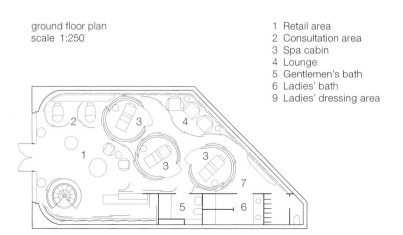

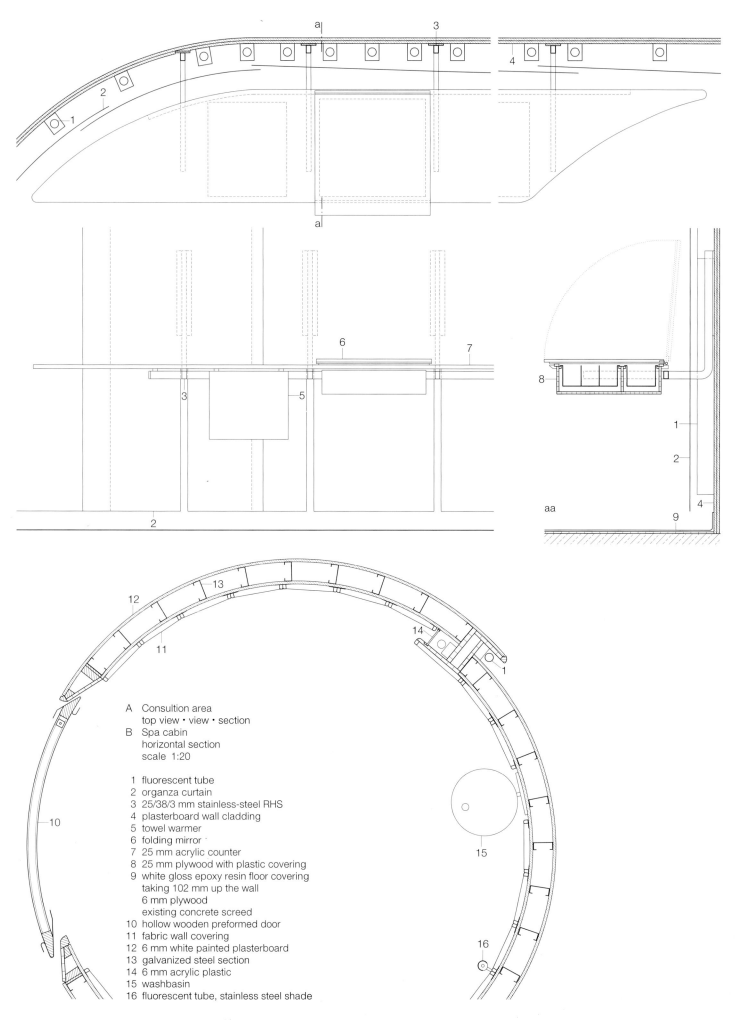

A Consultion area
top view · view · section

B Spa cabin
horizontal section
scale 1:20

1 fluorescent tube
2 organza curtain
3 25/38/3 mm stainless-steel RHS
4 plasterboard wall cladding
5 towel warmer
6 folding mirror
7 25 mm acrylic counter
8 25 mm plywood with plastic covering
9 white gloss epoxy resin floor covering
   taking 102 mm up the wall
   6 mm plywood
   existing concrete screed
10 hollow wooden preformed door
11 fabric wall covering
12 6 mm white painted plasterboard
13 galvanized steel section
14 6 mm acrylic plastic
15 washbasin
16 fluorescent tube, stainless steel shade

Fashion Shop in Vienna

Architects: propeller z, Vienna

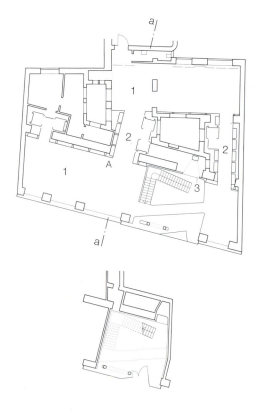

First floor plan
Ground floor plan
scale 1:400

1 Salesroom
2 Connecting corridor with shelves and
   changing-cubicles
3 Projection screen

The most striking feature of this Gil Boutique – oddly placed in a very busy Viennese shopping street – is the harmonious symbiosis of fashion and architecture. The concept is strictly minimalist, there is nothing undue or excessive, but it is precisely this that shows off the goods on offer so effectively. A little bar, a very fine sound system and a centrally placed screen for visual experiments produce a pleasant atmosphere that helps to put customers in the right mood. The old facade was removed down to the statically important components for the new shop in the remarkably short building period of two months. In the two-storey area, a tubular steel support carries the load of the of the building above, accentuating the entrance at the same time. The essentially uncomfortable fact of a small ground-floor area and a main sales area on the upper floor is managed very skilfully: a glazed facade section in front of the two-storey area is combined with the perforated glazing that fronts the whole of the upper floor, thus making the spatial situation intelligible from the outside. Inside, the vertical connection is made by opening up the floor. The upper sales areas are uniformly designed: light-coloured linoleum – rounded off at the corners – extends up the wall from the floor and continues on the ceiling. Shelves and changing-cubicles built of prefabricated plastic parts are installed in narrow connecting figures. The other furniture, which is used sparingly – display, storage and seating areas – is made of white, powder-coated materials and was also designed by the architect specially for the gil shop. The colour concept is very striking, a combination of intense yellow-green with shades of grey and white.

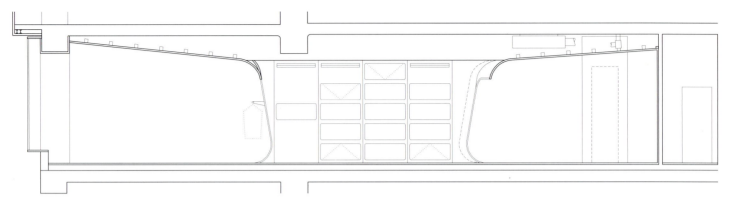

Section aa   scale 1:100

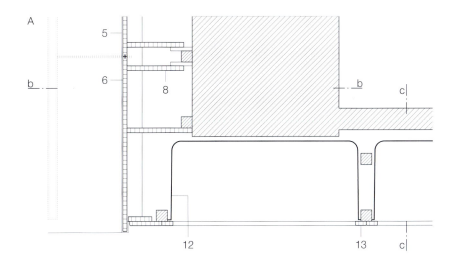

A

5

b

6

8

b

c

12

13

c

bb

cc

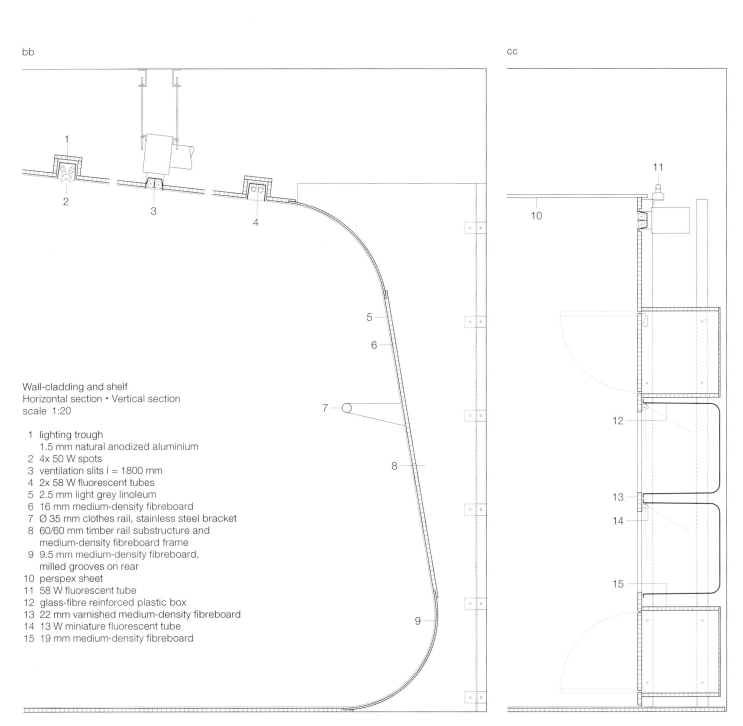

1

2

3

4

5

6

7

8

9

10

11

12

13

14

15

Wall-cladding and shelf
Horizontal section · Vertical section
scale 1:20

1 lighting trough
   1.5 mm natural anodized aluminium
2 4x 50 W spots
3 ventilation slits l = 1800 mm
4 2x 58 W fluorescent tubes
5 2.5 mm light grey linoleum
6 16 mm medium-density fibreboard
7 Ø 35 mm clothes rail, stainless steel bracket
8 60/60 mm timber rail substructure and
   medium-density fibreboard frame
9 9.5 mm medium-density fibreboard,
   milled grooves on rear
10 perspex sheet
11 58 W fluorescent tube
12 glass-fibre reinforced plastic box
13 22 mm varnished medium-density fibreboard
14 13 W miniature fluorescent tube
15 19 mm medium-density fibreboard

Fashion Shop in London

Architects: Future Systems, London

On being commissioned by the Italian fashion company Marni to develop a new concept for its shops, the architects decided to take couture as a source of inspiration for their design. The concept was to be applicable to individual shops as well as to the company's boutiques within large department stores. The actual articles of clothing, their texture, colours and composition provided the inspiration for the spatial design. This is based on the idea of an interior landscape in which clothes, shoes and accessories are essential components of the overall composition. In the London shop presented here, the floor, walls and ceiling are dark blue in colour, although this can be varied to match new collections or the changing seasons. The uniform coloration of the enclosing surfaces seems to dissolve the spatial contours. In the midst of this "ocean", the clothes are presented on a white, organically shaped island that "floats" 75 mm above the level of the floor. The form of the island is echoed by the polished stainless-steel suspended soffit in which the interior of the shop is reflected. As a result, one does not have the impression of standing in a rectilinear space. Articles of clothing and accessories hang decoratively from sculpturally shaped perspex hangers suspended from long, curved, stainless-steel arms. A further rail swings dynamically round the boutique, following the line of the island and broadening at its end to merge with a sales and display counter that describes a sine curve and appears to extend endlessly through the space. The cash desk is concealed beneath the polished metal top. Viewed from the street, the articles of clothing seem to draw the hangers and rails downwards, with the result that the organically flowing space appears to be in a state of movement.

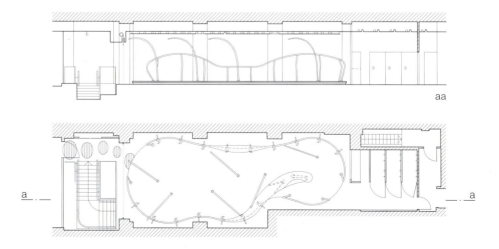

aa

a

a

Section • Plan
scale 1:250
Axonometric

92

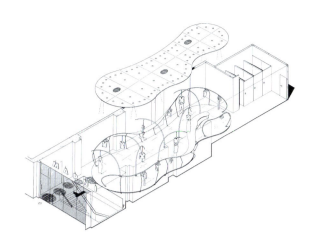

1 Ø 45 mm stainless-steel tube
2 Ø 35 mm stainless-steel tube
3 perspex coat hanger
4 15 mm stainless-steel plate
5 floor construction:
  17 mm crystalline flint-glass tiling
  8 mm levelling layer
  25 mm plywood
6 20 mm medium-density fibreboard fascia
7 2 mm sheet stainless steel welded to
  stainless-steel tube, with burnished finish
8 Ø 30 mm bored opening for electric cable
9 cable clip

Section   scale 1:20

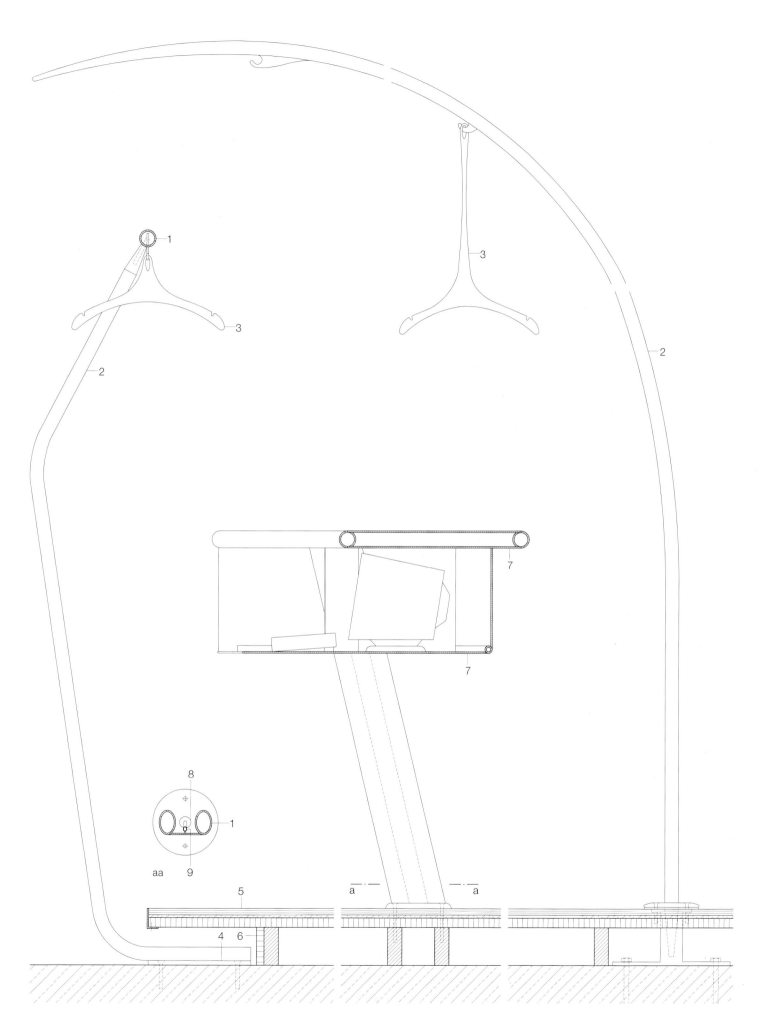

Supermarket in Wattens

Architects: Dominique Perrault, Paris
Reichert Pranschke Maluche, Munich

From the outside the building, which is sited opposite a much-visited glas factory and surrounded by an impressive mountain landscape, looks like a large, geometrical crystal. Customers can admire the imposing landscape from the inside through the sales shelves. The mountain chains are refracted in the opaque white panes of the glass facades. In the entrance area the facade abandons its austere geometry, steps backwards in an elegant curve and creates a space for a little piece of nature: birches and pines of the kind found in the surrounding mountain forests are incorporated in the architecture by a tall curving fence, thus blurring the transition between inside and outside. The green of the group of trees changes the quality of the daylight that penetrates the inside space, filtered by the white glass. This produces an internal quality that is quite extraordinary for a supermarket: natural light and the muted view of the outside world provide an interesting setting for the goods on offer. The interior design is special as well. The space derives its character from an austere, carefully detailed steel structure painted in dark colours. The artificial lighting picks up the orthogonal pattern of the girders. Continuous lighting strips in the ceiling provide even illumination, and suspended spotlights and individual lamps provide accents in the sales area. The massive exposed concrete backbone that makes up the facade facing the mountains makes it easier to find one's way around. The industrial-style shelves are designed to be low and transparent so that the overall size of the supermarket is still discernible and the space retains its generous scale.

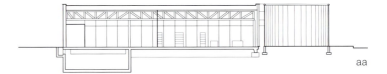

aa

bb

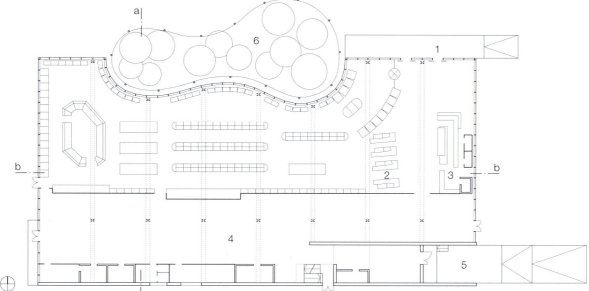

Floor plan
sections
scale 1:500

1 Entrance
2 Checkouts
3 Bar
4 Side rooms
5 Delivery
6 Green area

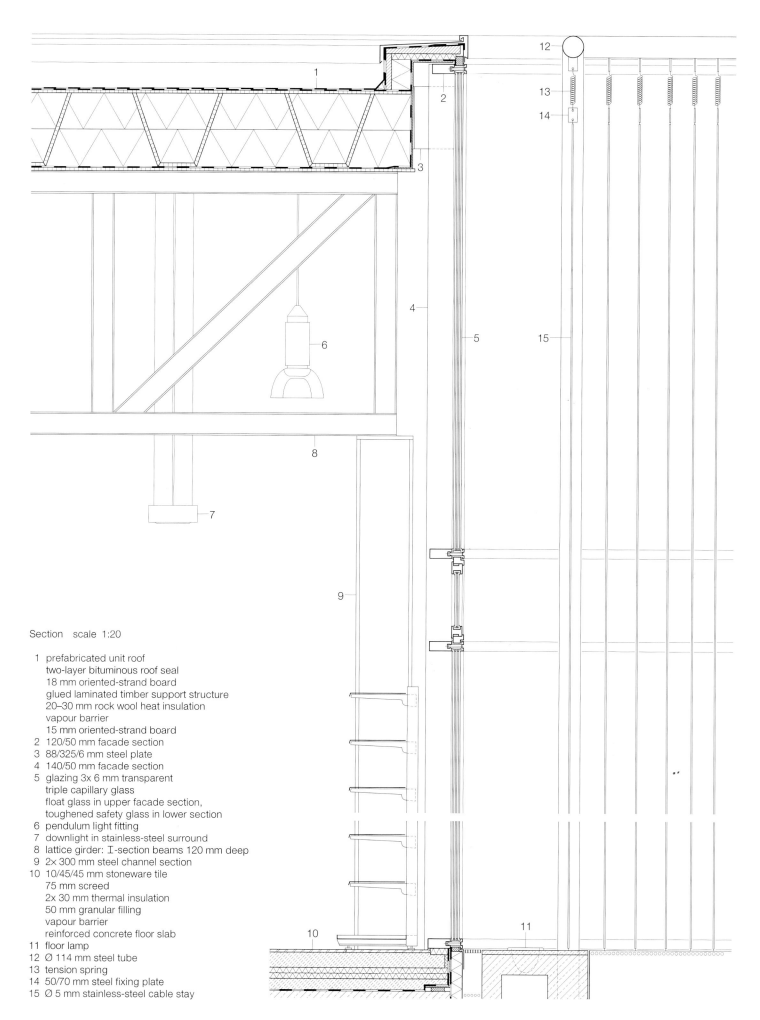

Section   scale 1:20

1 prefabricated unit roof
   two-layer bituminous roof seal
   18 mm oriented-strand board
   glued laminated timber support structure
   20–30 mm rock wool heat insulation
   vapour barrier
   15 mm oriented-strand board
2 120/50 mm facade section
3 88/325/6 mm steel plate
4 140/50 mm facade section
5 glazing 3x 6 mm transparent
   triple capillary glass
   float glass in upper facade section,
   toughened safety glass in lower section
6 pendulum light fitting
7 downlight in stainless-steel surround
8 lattice girder: I-section beams 120 mm deep
9 2x 300 mm steel channel section
10 10/45/45 mm stoneware tile
   75 mm screed
   2x 30 mm thermal insulation
   50 mm granular filling
   vapour barrier
   reinforced concrete floor slab
11 floor lamp
12 Ø 114 mm steel tube
13 tension spring
14 50/70 mm steel fixing plate
15 Ø 5 mm stainless-steel cable stay

Eat in/Take out Restaurant in Tokyo

Architects: Klein Dytham architecture, Tokyo

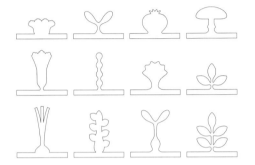

Healthy and trendy – the abstract symbols cut out of polyurethane have become a trade mark. They are lined up all
the away along the long shelves and decorate the completely
glazed facade of this takeaway restaurant in central Tokyo.
It caters for the young professionals in the Japanese capital
who spend hours in front of a flickering monitor and then want
to eat quickly but healthily in a pleasant atmosphere.
The green pictograms are in the shape of various vegetables
and catch the eye in this otherwise sparsely furnished
restaurant. The long rectangular ground plan is divided into
a restaurant and a service area. The latter is opposite the
entrance – customers who are in a hurry can place their
order here then take it away. Those with more time to spare
will go into the restaurant next to eat, which can seat up
to 40. Here the company logo is painted on the end wall, as
though intended to make people welcome. The wall opposite
the front window is clad in corrugated mirror glass. In front
of this, as on the street side, are shelves with the plastic
pictograms on them.
The furniture is kept simple and restrained, to form an appropriate framework for presenting the plastic vegetables. Each
of them has a magnet on its base, so that the arrangement
can be changed. The light that comes into the space is
reflected in the mirrored surface, which multiplies the abstract
vegetable decoration. This is a simple effect, but it enables
the architects to take the restaurant out into the street in visual
terms, at the same time giving the interior a bright and cheerful
atmosphere. The green of the pictograms harmonizes with the
bamboo wood used for the fittings. Counter, chairs, tables and
floor are all in this dark timber shade. Only the green-painted
bench running the full length of the rear wall picks up the
colour of the polyurethane figures.
The original intention was to have real grass on the shelves,
but plants have to be looked after, and so this idea was
rejected. The architects consulted the designer responsible
for the catering company, and this gave them the idea for the
easy-care plastic evergreen vegetables.

Section
floor plan
scale 1:100

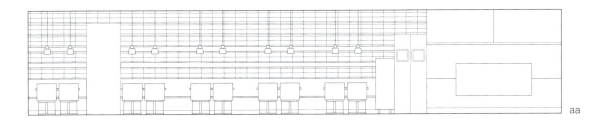

aa

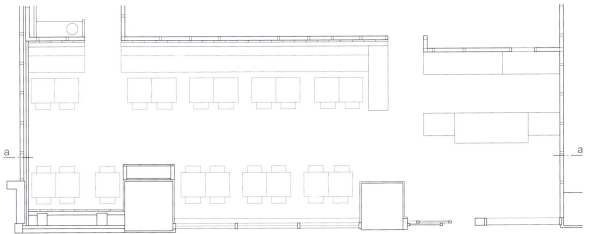

a

a

Rear wall
View · Section
scale 1:5
Section scale 1:20

1 12 mm plasterboard painted white
2 3 mm steel flat, reflective surface
   on 9 mm plasterboard
3 2x 12 mm plasterboard painted white
4 green acrylic cover
5 polyurethane upholstery
6 5 mm moulded plywood element
7 48/48 mm timber section
8 700/700/15 mm bamboo tabletop on
   500/500/3 mm steel plate
9 Ø 60 mm chromium-plated steel tube
10 3 mm reflective cladding
11 1820/91/15 mm bamboo floorboards

12 303/305 mm corrugated plastic mirror panel
   fastened to 13 with adhesive tape
13 30/12 timber section
14 green polyurethane vegetable figure
   underside magnetic
15 3 mm steel flat painted green
16 12/12 mm timber section
17 9 mm plywood
18 5 mm bamboo cladding
19 fluorescent tube
20 18/18/2 mm steel angle
   painted white
21 3 mm translucent acrylic glass

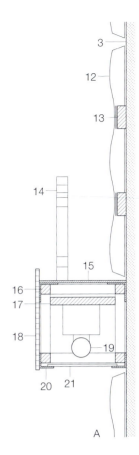

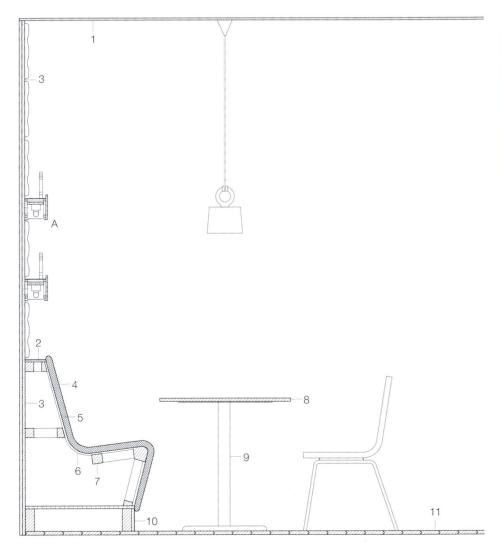

Brasserie in New York

Architects: Diller + Scofidio, New York

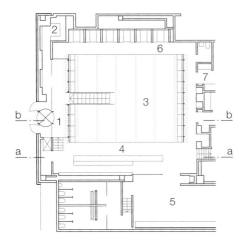

As part of the interior design and fitting out of Ludwig Mies van der Rohe's Seagram Building (1954–58), Philip Johnson created the Four Seasons restaurant and a brasserie in the basement. The brasserie was destroyed by fire some years ago and has since been redesigned by the New York architects Diller and Scofidio.

The new dining space, set more than a metre below the entrance level, is dominated by the use of pear plywood elements. It is linked with the foyer by a glass staircase that dramatizes the entrance of visitors as if they were walking onstage. At one end, the staircase slices through the wooden shell-like elements that line the narrower faces of the dining space. Along the side wall to the left of the stairs is a series of dining recesses. On the opposite side of the brasserie is the bar, the rear wall of which has been designed as a room-height illuminated hollow space in which the various drinks are displayed. The wall comprises a fascia of sliding, translucent glass elements, behind which bottle-holders are fixed in front of rear-lighted translucent panels. Behind the bar is a smaller, separate restaurant area.

The atmosphere of the brasserie is largely determined by the continuous strip of wooden elements with which it is fitted out. Their curved forms help to relieve the plain, sober quality of the orthogonal space. At its base, the slightly inclined wall lining flows into the bentwood surfaces of the seating; at the top, it curves round to link up with the lapped soffit elements. The timber strip flooring also curves up at the edges to merge with the seating.

An important aspect of the interior design is the social ritual of seeing and being seen. Every visitor is filmed on entering the building, and the images are automatically relayed to the first of 15 LCD screens suspended over the bar, so that the arrival of guests is announced before they actually enter the restaurant area. At the same time, a screen in the cloakroom allows arriving guests to observe passers-by in the street outside. Within a very short time, the brasserie has managed to establish links with its illustrious past and has become a fashionable venue in New York's nightlife.

Plan of restaurant
scale 1:400
Sections through
restaurant
scale 1:250

1 Entrance
2 Cloakroom
3 Restaurant
4 Bar
5 Small dining room
6 Dining recesses
7 Kitchen

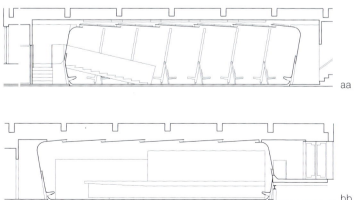

aa

bb

LED lights

Sectional details   scale 1:10

1 25 mm pear-veneered moulded plywood element
2 frosted-glass cover strip
3 90 mm stainless-steel channel section
4 stainless-steel support: two flats 13.5 mm wide tapering to 9 mm at top
5 110/110/10 mm stainless-steel angles bolted to both sides of primary supporting member and to entrance landing
6 60/60/6 mm stainless-steel angles bolted to both sides of primary supporting member
7 60/60/6 mm steel angle
8 EPDM intermediate layer
9 stainless-steel bracket bolted to supporting member
10 stainless-steel plate welded to base plate and supporting member
11 13.5 x 13.5 mm stainless-steel plate
12 floor construction:
    20 mm hardwood strip flooring on
    40/60 mm bearers
    60 mm mineral filling as thermal insulation
13 stainless-steel purpose-made fixing
14 25 mm perforated pear-veneered plywood element
15 fluorescent lighting strip
16 air-conditioning outlet

A Sectional details of
seating recess
scale 1:10

1 steel section bolted
to concrete floor slab
2 stainless-steel cover strip
3 60/30/5 mm steel angle
4 plywood sheet screwed
to steel angles
5 51/51/6.3 mm steel SHS
6 65 mm steel channel
section
7 60 mm steel T-section
8 vinyl upholstery
9 hand-worked stainless-
steel section
10 Ø 100 mm stainless-
steel foot

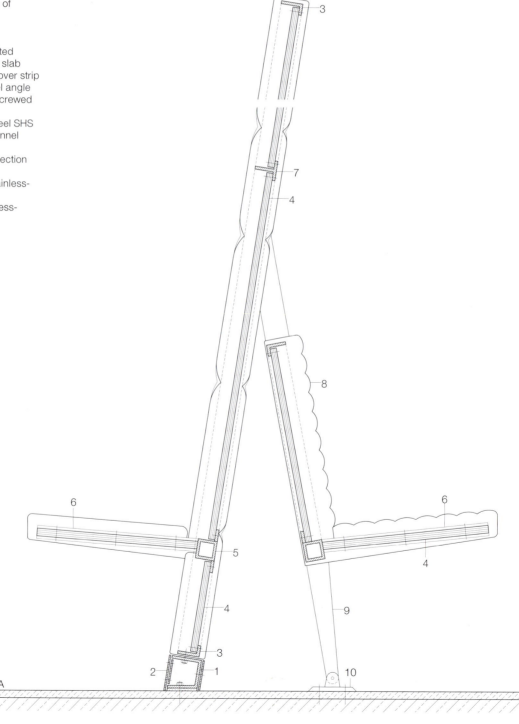

B Section through staircase
scale 1:100
C Sectional detail of stairs
scale 1:10

1 laminated safety glass
treads and risers:
2× 8 mm toughened glass
2 100 mm stainless-steel
channel section
3 stainless-steel string
4 laminated safety glass
balustrade: 2× 12 mm
toughened glass
5 20 mm terrazzo flooring

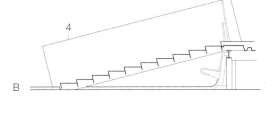

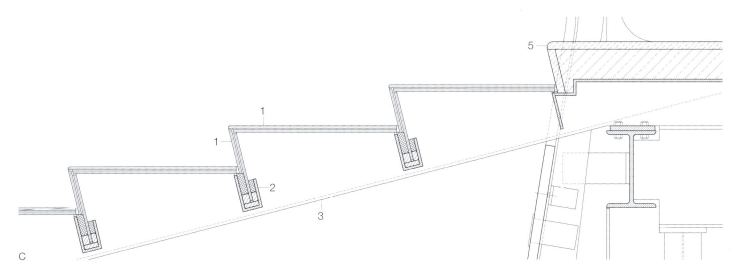

Bar in Heidelberg

Architects: liquid architektur/landschaft, Darmstadt

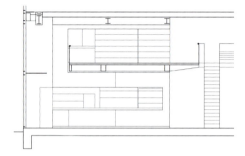

The matt, shimmering glow of this cube attracts hurrying night-time passers-by like moths to a candle-flame. This bar in the foyer of the Heidelberg printing press manufacturing company's headquarters is opposite the main station in Heidelberg. It attracts a lot of travellers in to relax for a while – and not just to kill time when they're waiting for a train. The lighting concept underlines the change of function: this section is a later addition to the nine-storey-high foyer of the Heidelberg offices. It functions as a café and bistro during the day and becomes a bar and lounge in the evening. Although it is an integral part of the reception and events area, it is run by an independent operator. This independence is expressed in the way the space is organized. The architects have "clamped" the daytime bar on the ground floor and the lounge at the upper level together. The figure fits around the ceiling structure of the existing gallery level like a large band. The glass cube stands out as a clear form, yet still responds to the individual zones' different requirements: it encloses the bar area on the ground floor, it becomes a large signal-like panel in the exterior space on the side that faces the main facade, and then on the gallery level for the lounge, which is furnished with couches, it frames this area and forms a spatial conclusion. 10 mm thick panes of toughened safety glass are mounted on a steel structure at the front, with reflecting surfaces at the back.

The three different colours used for the lights in the intermediate space plunge the body of the bar into alternating red, green or blue light, thus reinforcing the three-dimensional effect. The rear walls of the two bar areas are made up of red aluminium sheeting, in tones that harmonize with the colour of the furniture and fittings. The reduced design of the furniture, which is in different shades of red, complements the clear language of the interior finish, whose reticence achieves a three-dimensional quality, contrasting pleasingly with the excessively large and directionless architecture of the foyer zone, which rises through nine floors.

Section	1 Bar
Floor plans	2 Foyer
Entrance level	3 Lounge
Gallery level	4 Air space
scale 1:250	5 Gallery

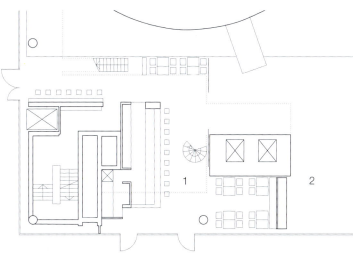
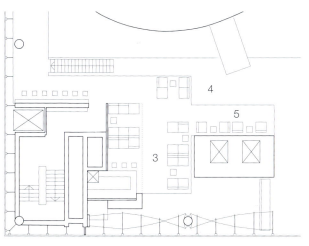

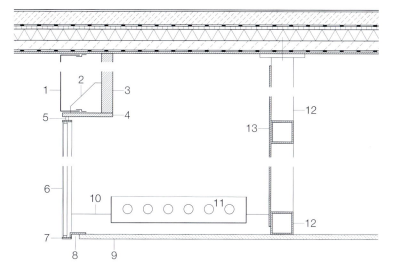

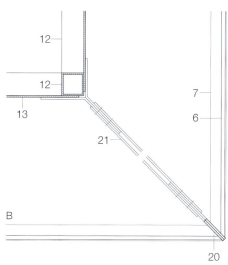

B

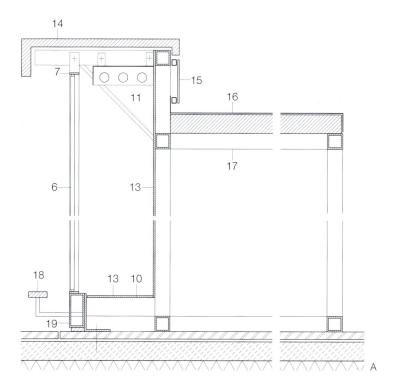

A

A Bar, ground floor
vertical section
B Corner detail
horizontal section
scale 1:10

1 1.55 mm polished stainless steel sheet
2 10 mm flat steel reinforcement
3 existing steel bearer
4 10 mm steel flats welded to existing bearer
5 threaded rod
6 10 mm toughened glass, rear coated
with matt foil
7 25/5 mm stainless steel frame inside coated
with light-scattering foil
8 shadow joint with aluminium angle
9 12.5 mm plasterboard suspended soffit
10 50/5 mm steel flat
11 fluorescent tubes in RGB colours
12 supporting structure 60/60 mm steel SHS
13 5 mm aluminium composite panel coated
with reflecting foil
14 black-painted beech bar counter
15 4 mm white acrylic plastic
16 1 mm stainless steel bar covering
on 40 mm chipboard
17 supporting structure 40/40 mm steel RHS
18 50/15 mm stainless steel plate foot grid
19 80/40 mm stainless steel
20 50/5 mm stainless steel plate to complete 6
21 Spacer 50/5 mm stainless steel plate
coated with reflecting foil

115

Office Bar in Tokyo

Architects: Klein Dytham architecture, Tokyo

The offices of the Australian financial services provider AMP are in the Tokyo business district of Roppongi. As office space is scarce and expensive, Klein Dytham organized workplaces, meeting rooms, reception, waiting area and bar on a single level. The budget and time-frame were both very constrained, which led to a most unusual, and thus particularly interesting spatial concept. Visitors to the office are immediately confronted with the large curved sliding elements that act as room dividers to separate the open office area behind them from the entrance. The counter in the entrance performs three functions: during the day it is simply part of the reception and waiting area for clients, or a kitchen for employees, but later on, when the roller elements have been opened up, it can be used as a bar. These curved sections set the tone for the whole space. Their red covering suggests the Australian landscape and also features in the client's company logo. And red makes a positive impression in Japan as well. The construction is as simple as it is innovative – thin nylon fabric covers a curved aluminium tube that is fastened to plastic rollers at its upper and lower ends. The room divider is made up of three elements whose height is staggered so that they can be pushed one inside the other. When you're sitting underneath them it seems as though there's a red canopy curving over the bar, which thus feels very intimate. The shape and colour signal the three possible uses of the space very clearly. When it is open it produces a screened-off area that clearly separates work and reception, and when the sections are pushed together the bar, with photo-wallpaper suggesting an atmosphere of leisure, opens up to offer employees a relaxed evening.

Section
scale 1:50

Track at top
wheel at bottom
scale 1:5

1 50 mm plastic wheel
2 ▱ 4.5 mm steel flat
3 12 mm plasterboard
    on steel substructure
4 2 mm aluminium track
5 aluminium tube Ø 25/2 mm
6 covering stretch nylon
7 90 mm plastic wheel

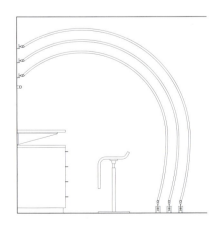

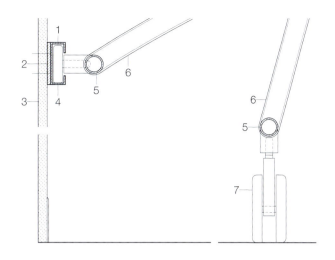

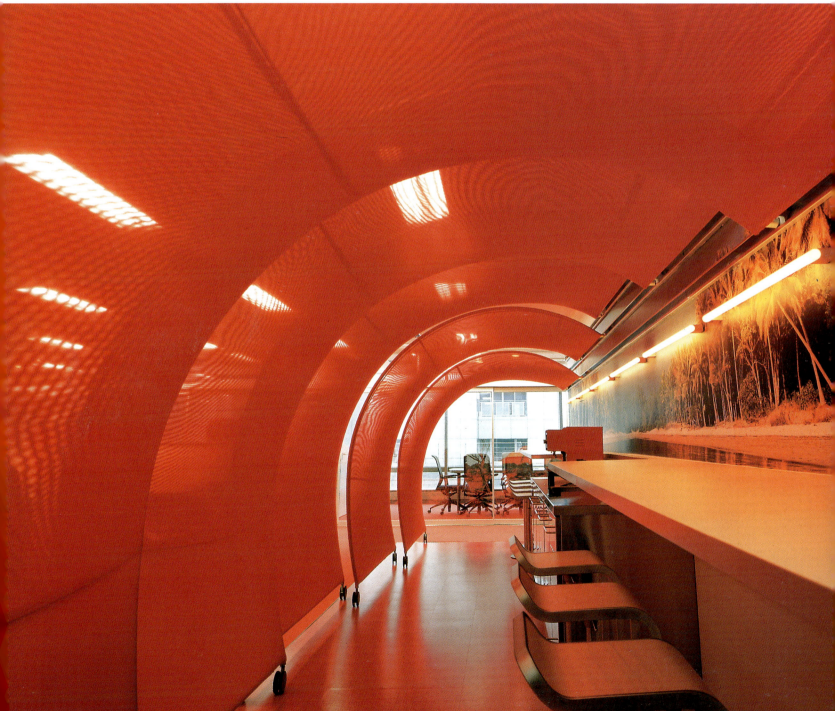

Architects' Office in Berlin

Architects: Nietz Prasch Sigl Tchoban Voss, Berlin

A shadowy hint of the interior organization can discerned from the outside through the U-section glass. The translucent walls close off the meeting area on the first floor of this architectural practice, organized on two levels, very inconspicuously. The glass cube placed directly behind the reception area screens off the workplaces that are to be found in the adjacent and larger section of the space. The practice is in a distinguished building complex in central Berlin, the Hackesche Höfe, whose characteristic brick architecture does not only define the exterior space. White-rendered walls and simple furnishings reveal the old structure of the building, the interior is reticent in its design. Only the meeting room and the steel staircase that links the two levels internally are particularly assertive features. It is not unusual for U-section glass to be used in interiors, but it is new for the individual elements to be installed horizontally and not vertically. The side of the glass box facing the corridor has a sliding door, and the two walls at the sides of it are attached to the external wall and adopt its orientation. The double building glass is held by angles at the ends and attached to a continuous aluminium section support structure. Inside, individual lengths of U-section glass are fastened to the wall element to present plan material. The lighting on this level is also discreet and appropriate to the working environment. The meeting room has a light-diffusing ceiling in foil, which provides even illumination along with the incident daylight.

plan entrance level   scale 1:400

1 Entrance
2 Reception
3 Meetings
4 Office
5 Archives

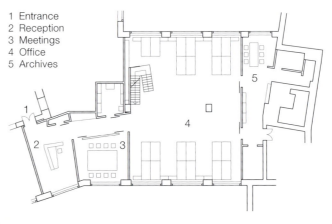

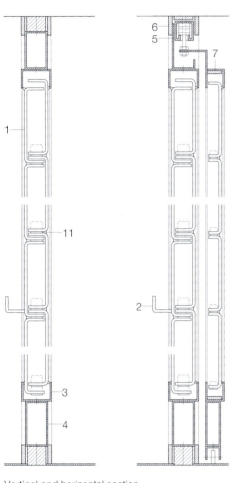

Vertical and horizontal section
scale 1:10

1 U-section glass etched on
  the outside, 25/60/7 mm
2 Plan bracket U-section glass
3 Frame aluminium section
4 120/60 cm steel RHS
5 Runner for sliding door
6 Lacquered aluminium strip
7 40/8 mm steel insert
8 aluminium angle
9 80/50/3 mm aluminium
  channel frame, screwed to 10
10 50/50/5 mm steel stay
11 Bearer glass section 30/30 mm
  with silicone bearing

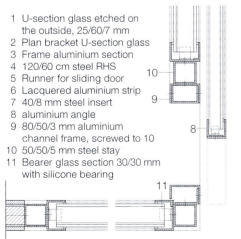

Agency in Munich

Architects: lynx architecture, Munich
with tools off. architecture, Munich

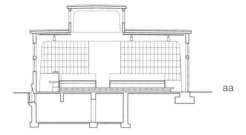

aa

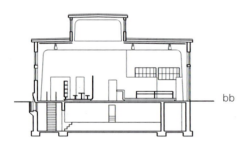

bb

There is nothing to suggest to visitors coming in to the back yard from the street that there is a lavishly designed workspace in the former industrial hall. Large wooden doors extend over the whole courtyard facade, and when they are open, you can look into the interior of the hall: plain tables and benches made of solid wood stand on a large reinforced concrete slab that looks as though it is floating above the floor; its sides, folding up and then out at right angles, conclude the area and function as a counter and a boundary at the same time. People sit here and there at the tables, reading, eating or talking; the Munich Agency's cafeteria is one of the three inserted function areas that structure the space. The existing, listed building was refurbished and left in its original condition to preserve its character. The floor is covered with a colourless matt seal, and still shows signs of its earlier use. The building was originally constructed as a lorry factory hall. The space is almost 6 m high, and creates a light, pleasant working atmosphere, with continuous roof-lights in the side walls and lantern. Double-hinged frames make up the load-bearing structure and at the same time articulate the space, which is divided into a large and a small section by the raised former masters' cabins.

The workplaces are in the larger section, on a felt-covered wooden platform. Like the cafeteria, it is raised as if on a plinth and thus detaches itself from the existing building as a large inserted item of furniture. The workspaces are placed on the wooden structure, separated by a corridor running down the middle, and made into rows by shelves; shelves also close off the ends of the area. Both the wiring and the convectors that complement the existing radiators are installed in the plinth. The Agency's library, which is formed by a 8 m long angle of untreated, rusting steel, is in the smaller section opposite the library café. On the open side, the section that is folded upwards forms a kind of screen that shelters the reading area behind it from everything else that is going on in the building. The architects have deliberately used design and also their chosen materials to set the inserted elements that create the space off from the existing hall – the new is placed inside the old and preserves its original character. Even the wood-wool sheets that have been installed for acoustical reasons are placed inconspicuously between the individual ribs of the load-bearing structure on the underside of the ceilings.

Sections
Ground floor plan
scale 1:400

1 Reception
2 Open-plan office
3 Conference room
4 Cafeteria
5 Library

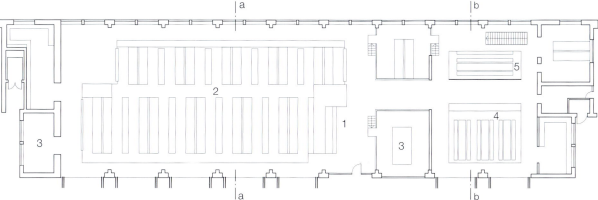

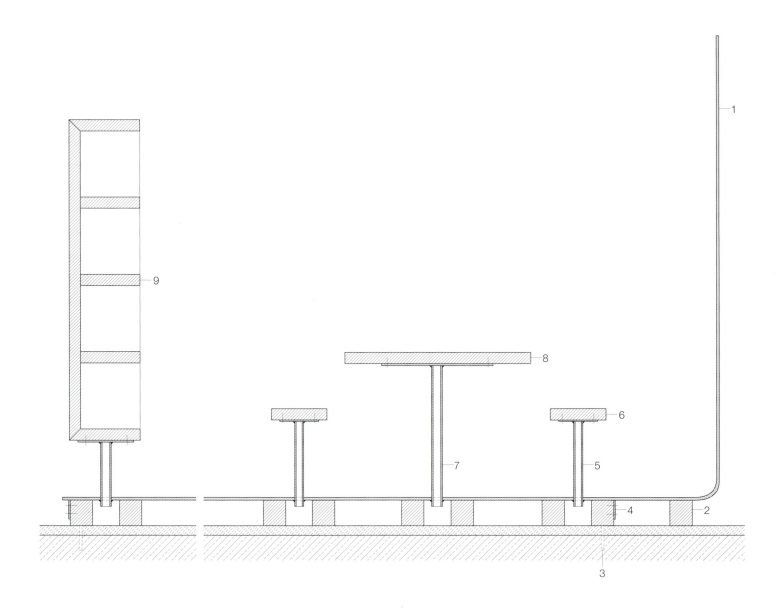

Library section
Reception section
scale 1:20

1 untreated 15 mm steel angle
   vertical section leaning 10 mm
   inwards at the top
2 140/120 mm wood bearer
3 M 12 bonding anchor
4 8 mm steel plate screwed to wood bearer
5 48.3 mm dia. steel tube 7.1 mm thick
   pushed through and welded underneath
6 60 mm solid maple bench
7 57 mm dia. steel tube 8 mm thick
   pushed through and welded underneath
8 60 mm untreated solid maple table-top
9 60 mm untreated solid maple bookcase
10 100/100 mm wood bearer
11 100/10 mm steel angle
12 100/70 mm wood bearer
13 25 mm oriented-strand board
   with felt covering
14 stand structure made up
   of 50/50/5 mm steel SHS
15 19 mm plywood sheeting covered with felt
16 15 mm veneered plywood sheet
   with black plastic coating

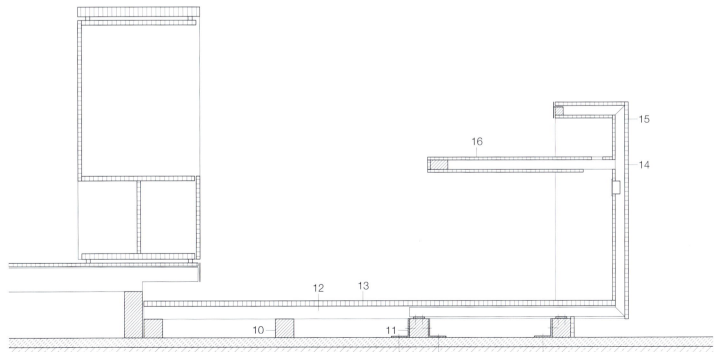

Royal Library in Copenhagen

Architects: Schmidt, Hammer & Lassen, Copenhagen

The Royal Library extension is prominently placed by Copenhagen harbour. The existing historic brick building was extended by the addition of a narrow new block in 1969, and this has now been integrated into the new building. The new cuboid seems monolithic from the outside: it is called the "black diamond" because of its highly polished granite facade and inclined edges. The new building picks up the old library's access line and continues it in the form of an atrium rising through the full height of the complex. The actual entrance visitors use to enter the foyer is on the southern narrow side. This area includes a restaurant, as well as an events venue and a bookshop. A two storey spiral section clad in grey sandstone, adjacent to the north, accommodates other functions. The actual library extension begins on the first floor, and is connected to the old building by a broad bridge housing the lending facilities. The reading rooms extend over two floors and face the atrium, and there are more workplaces on the inserted gallery levels, which gain additional daylight from roof-lights. Built-in ceiling spots provide dazzle-free lighting after dark. Table lamps designed especially for the library provide auxiliary illumination at the individual workplaces. The interior is dominated by sandstone, exposed concrete and maple-wood, and these light-coloured materials underline the generosity of the interior space. Lights pours into the public areas from the high windows and this, combined with the delicate colouring and clean lines, gives an impression of space and comfort. The furniture is uniform in all areas. Whether you are in the reading rooms, the restaurant or the bookshop – the fittings are simply designed and form an agreeable contrast with the expressive formal language of the building.

Ground plan of floor with reading room
Scale 1:1000

1 Reading room
2 Newspaper reading area
3 Microfiche area
4 Office
5 Lending facilities

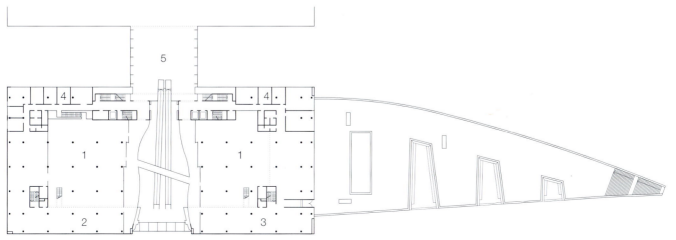

125

Table in the reading room
Sections · Top view   scale 1:10

1 5 mm safety glass set on its edge
2 lamp 20/40 mm aluminium section, turns and tilts,
   upper section solid with integrated illumination, lower section tubular
3 flexible book support:
   10 mm safety glass, stainless steel support
   and power-point housing
4 14 mm maple parquet tabletop, 16 mm medium-density fibreboard
   edges solid maple strip
5 supporting structure 40/60 mm steel tubes
6 cable duct
7 computer cupboard below, support structure 15/15 mm steel tube
8 door 1 mm aluminium sheet with magnetic catch, painted outside,
   covered with felt inside (sound insulation)
9 door painted medium-density fibreboard with magnetic catch
10 number-plate brushed stainless steel, numbers engraved
11 groove to mark individual places

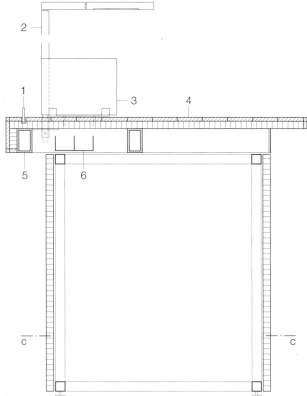

aa

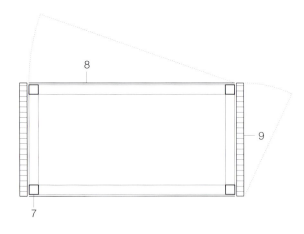

cc

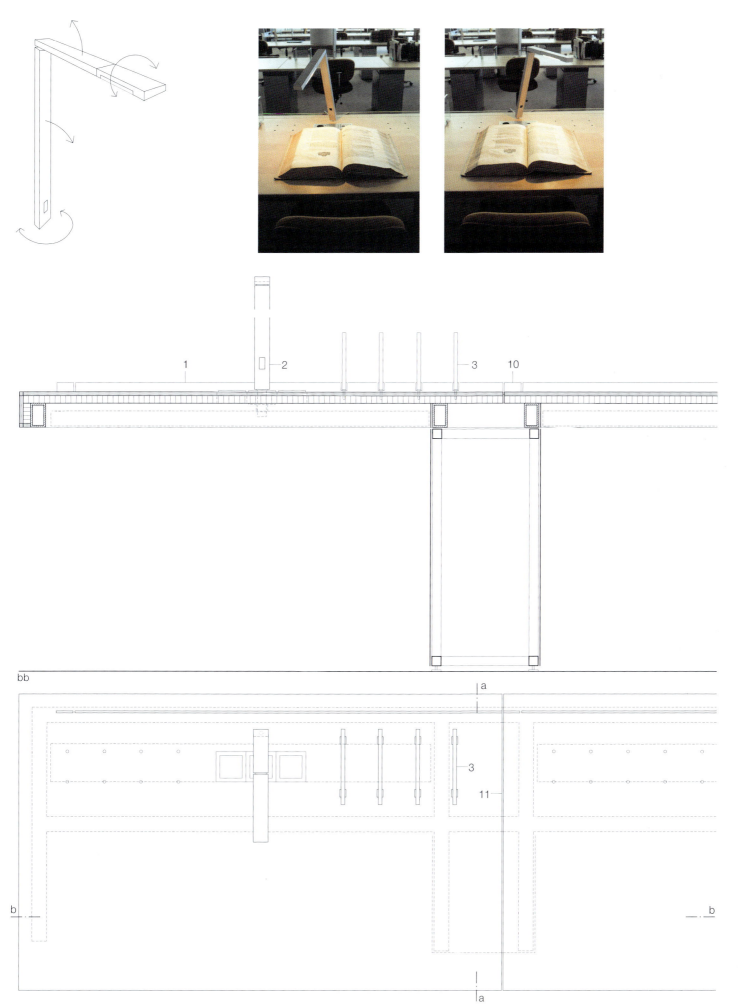

1
2
3
10

bb

a

3

11

b   b

a

National Library of France in Paris

Architects: Dominique Perrault, Paris, in collaboration with Gaëlle Lauriot-Prévost

The interior of the Bibliothèque Nationale in Paris is distinguished by its surface qualities, which manifest themselves in simple forms and textures in combination with a restrained coloration and an unusual use of materials. The six storeys of the complex that are located partly underground beneath the esplanade extend between the outer corners of the towers and house the areas accessible to the public: reception, information centre, reading rooms and ancillary functions. The 12 storeys in each of the towers accommodate book stores and space for the archivists and librarians.

The interior design is articulated by the colours of the materials used: each functional area thus has its own specific character. The public zones are in red, ochre and silver, while the spaces for special events are in red and black tones. The circulation areas are dominated by the silver of the metal curtains. The dramatically staged lines of access to and from the reading rooms are 30 m high and 5 m wide. Hung with large metallic "tapestries", they evoke associations of medieval cathedrals. The fitting out of the reading rooms, on the other hand, is characterized by a quality of restraint. The strict geometry of the wood furnishings and finishings creates an atmosphere of calm and concentration. Here, in contrast to the circulation areas, it is the load-bearing structure that determines the spatial impression: the concrete piers and downstand beams are left visible and serve to articulate the space.

The interior is distinguished by the use of clear forms and natural colours, which create a restrained background to the rows of plain, unadorned tables and chairs. The reading tables are arranged in such a way that visitors enjoy a view out to the courtyard with its large pine trees. The furnishings were also developed by the architects: the designs for the chairs, benches, tables, shelving and light fittings are derived from simple basic forms, to which different elements may be added, depending on the required function. The various kinds of stainless-steel fabric that were used – normally found in filter, aeronautic and space technology – serve here as acoustic wall and soffit hangings. They conceal service installations and are used as framed or tensioned lightweight partitions and as sliding sunscreens. The harmonious interplay between wood, stainless steel and concrete, together with the surface coloration and the careful detailing, lend the spaces a calm, noble appearance.

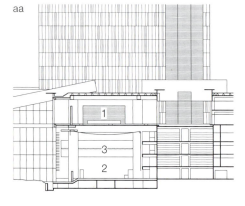

aa

Part section aa
scale 1:1000
Plan · Longitudinal section
scale 1:4000

1 Public reading rooms
2 Reading hall for research work
3 Suspended reading rooms
  for valuable books

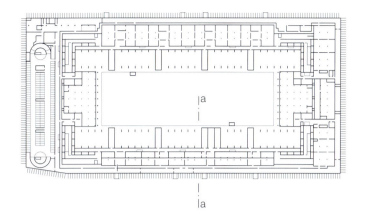

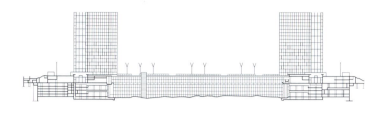

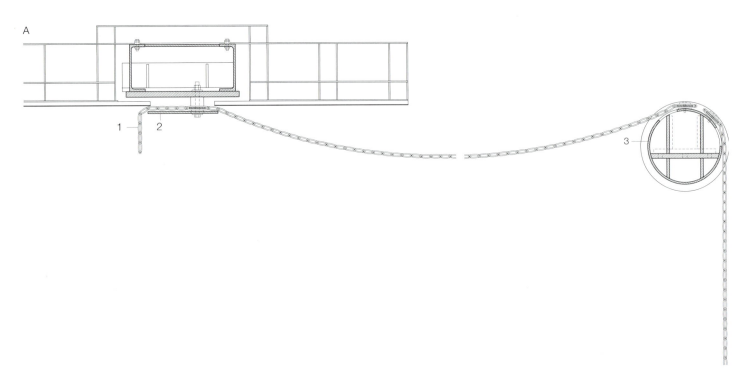

A   Suspended soffit in reading room
     Vertical section   scale 1:20
B   Metal grille to narrow faces of towers
     Internal elevation
     Vertical section
     scale 1:50
     Vertical and horizontal sectional details
     scale 1:10

1   stainless-steel mesh
2   380/10 mm stainless-steel plate
3   Ø 400/10 mm stainless-steel tube
4   150/150/8 mm steel mesh
5   stainless-steel looped mesh
6   120/40/8 mm steel RHS
7   slip connection
8   steel tensioning spring

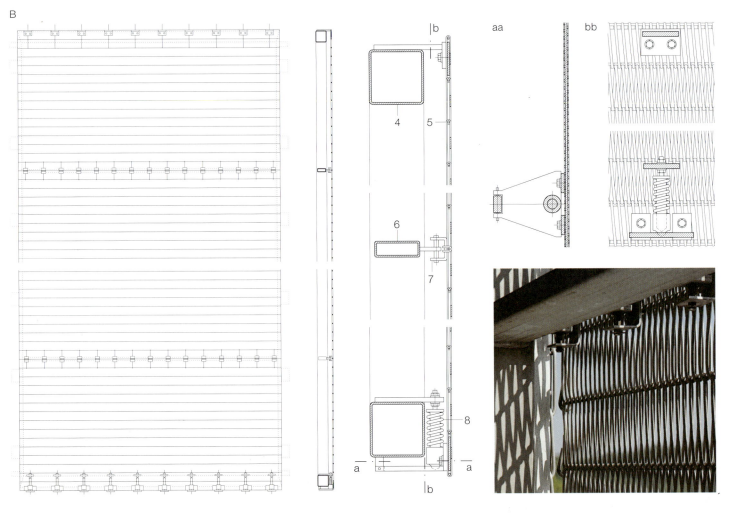

132

Single-arm table lamp
Axonometric
Exploded diagram

Tate Modern in London

Architects: Herzog & de Meuron, Basel

Enjoy the view of the Thames over cup of tea after an exciting walk round the exhibition – the restaurant on the top floor of Tate Modern is already an attraction in its own right. The room is restrained in its furnishings, and framed by the poster-effect rear wall and the outsize letters on the windows. The great experience for visitors is the panoramic view of London through the floor-to-ceiling glazing in the light beam that the architects have placed on top of the building.

The former Bankside Power Station, built by Sir Giles Gilbert Scott in 1945, now contains one of the largest modern art collections. The building in organized in three parallel tracts: on the Thames side is the boiler-house, in the middle is the huge turbine hall and on the south side the switch house, which still has the transformers in it. Access to this section is a possible option for the gallery, and arrangements for its conversion were included in the original design. This will considerably enhance the facilities available, and also add to the already powerful impact made by the building. A broad ramp on the west side leads down into the cathedral-like turbine hall, which extends over full length and height of the building. On the left is the new facade of the museum section, with showcase-style balconies that look like floating light sources. Here the individual exhibition levels thrust out into the hall, linking art and public life and turning the visitors into exhibits. On the opposite side the facade is completely closed – the spaces behind it will be added to the museum at a later date. The bridge above the main area is the remains of a floor slab that originally ran the full length of the building. It was removed so that visitors could experience the full scale of the former turbine hall. The bridge leads visitors into the museum section with its galleries. The individual galleries differ in their dimensions and proportions, and provide exhibition space for a whole range of material. Daylight comes into the interior through roof lights and the gigantic windows. The outside views make it easier to find one's way about, and offer attractive views of central London. Continuous lighting strips, which can scarcely be distinguished from the skylights in their design and light intensity, are set in the plasterboard ceilings and provide additional artificial lighting that can be very finely regulated for the galleries.

The great glowing volume floating above the heavy brick building and admitting daylight to the gallery floors lights up the London sky with artificial light at night. This light beam conducts a dialogue with the 93-metre high tower, and has become an impressive emblem of the museum.

Plans
Section
scale 1:2000

Grand staircase
A Longitudinal section
  scale 1:50
B Balustrade detail
  cross-section
  scale 1:10

1 West entrance with ramp
2 Public concourse
  (former Turbine Hall)
3 Bookshop
4 Educational facilities
5 Information and tickets
6 Oil tanks (disused)
7 Bridge
8 Café
9 Auditorium and
  seminar rooms
10 Store
11 Switch house
12 Galleries
13 Void over galleries
14 Restaurant

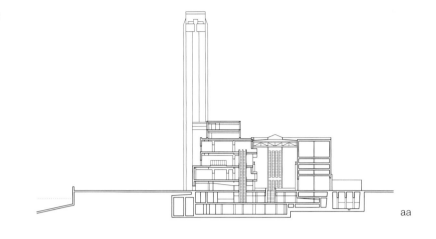

aa

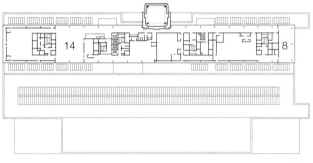

level 7

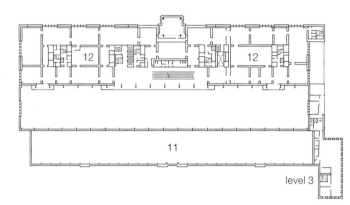

level 3

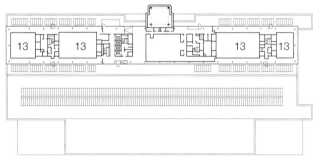

level 6

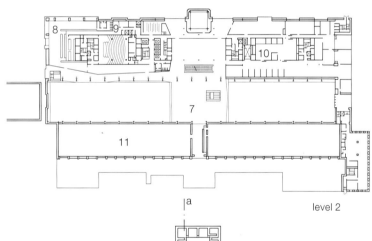

level 2

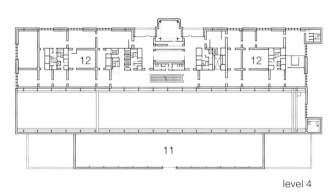

level 4

level 1

1 steel I-section carriage
2 steel channel
  cross-members in plane
  of staircase flight
3 sheet-steel treads and
  risers bent to shape
4 25 mm untreated oak treads
  on 12 mm plywood
5 steel channel members in
  plane of balustrade
6 sheet-steel lining, painted
7 hardwood handrail
8 fluorescent tube

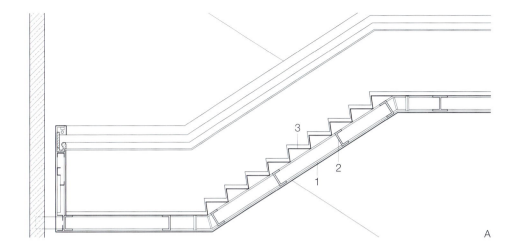

A

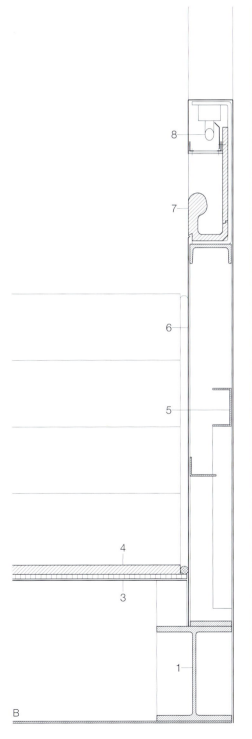

B

sections
scale 1:50
details
scale 1:10

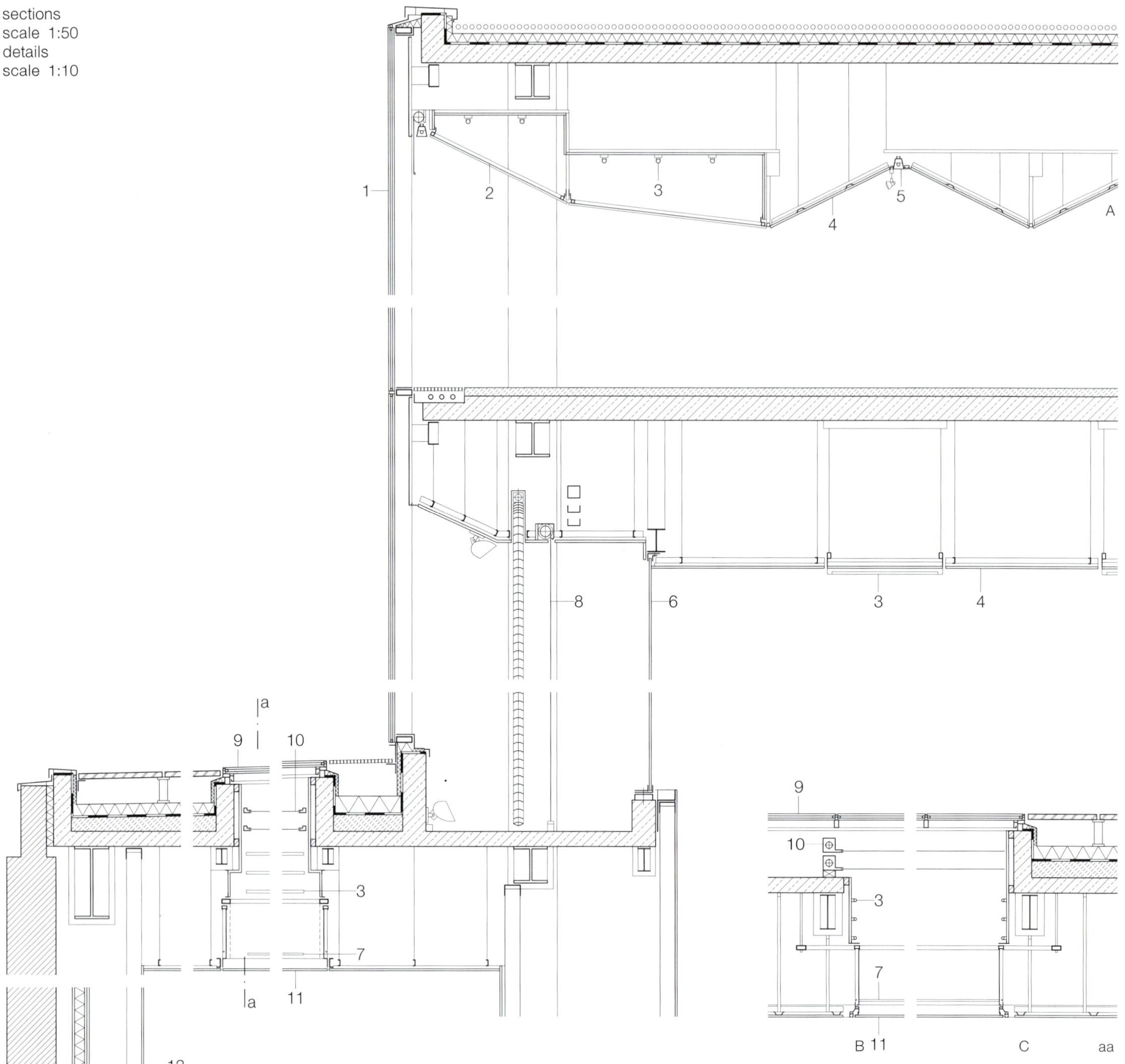

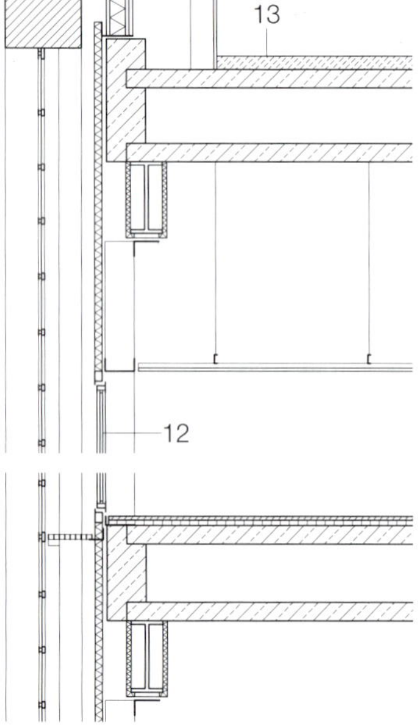

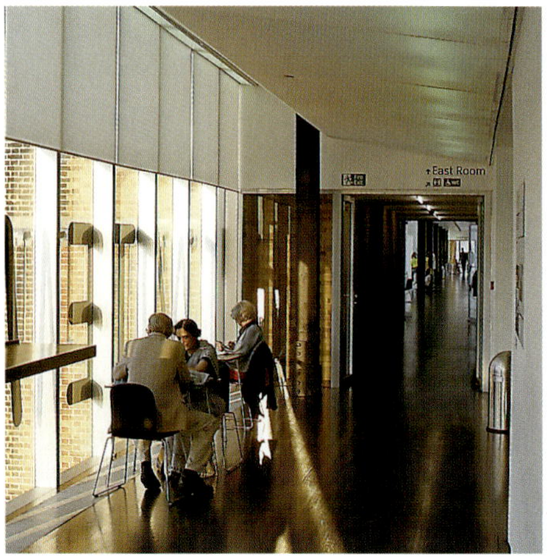

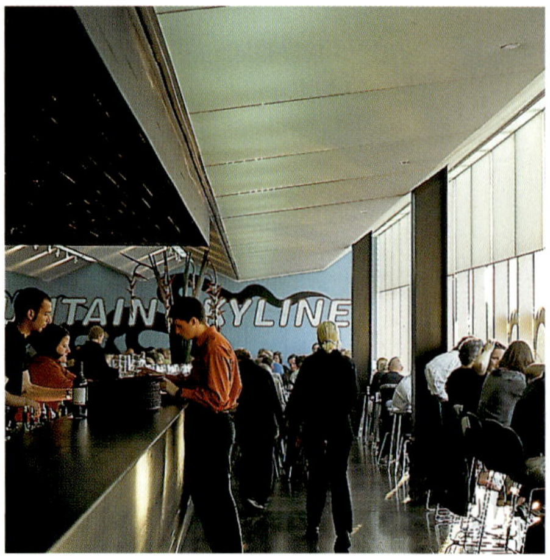

1

2

3

5

4

A

8

6

3

4

|a

9 | 10

3

7

|a

11

13

12

9

10

3

7

B 11   C   aa

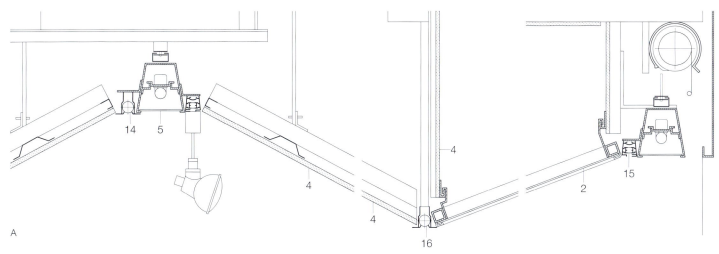

A

1 alum. facade with double glazing: 18 mm safety glass; 15 mm cavity; 12 mm lam. safety glass
2 2 mm fabric lining
3 fluorescent tube
4 plasterboard on supporting structure
5 lightning rail with integrated sprinkler heads
6 22 mm lam. safety glass clerestory to gallery
7 polycarbonate diffuser with sanded face
8 fabric anti-glare screen
9 roof light: 8 mm toughened glass; 15 mm cavity; 12 mm lam. safety glass; with opal PVB layer
10 motor-operated fabric blind
11 10 mm bead-blasted lam. safety glass with opal PVB intermediate layer
12 24 mm double glazing (G 30)
13 75 mm anthracite-coloured screed
14 air outlet
15 aluminium lightning rail
16 extruded aluminium section

ceiling galleries
scale 1:10

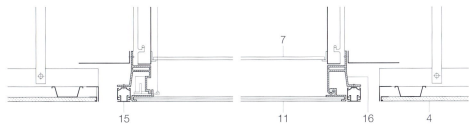

B

C

145

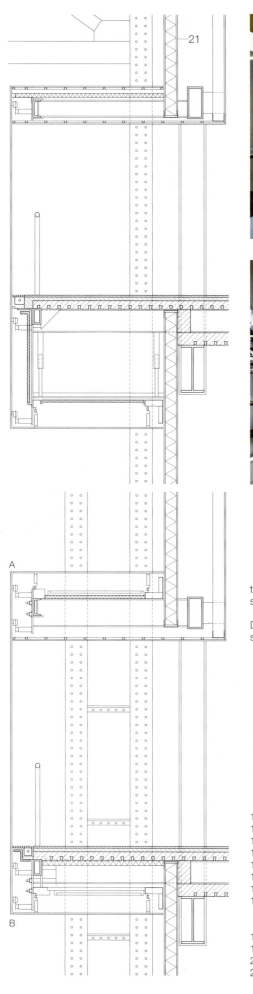

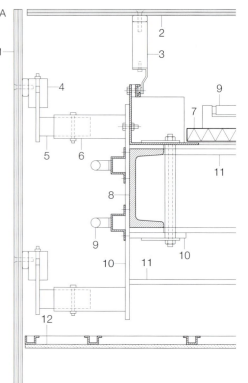

A

1

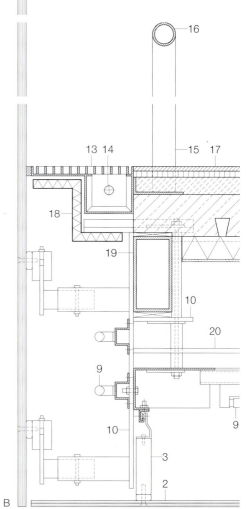

turbine hall
scale 1:50

Details balconies
scale 1:10

 1 22 mm lam. safety glass with
    sandblasted outer face and
    opal epoxy-resin-coated inner face
 2 sliding element: 13 mm lam. safety glass
    with sandblasted outer face
 3 68 mm dia. aluminium tube
 4 75/50/46 mm milled steel element
 5 50/50/6 mm steel SHS with
    130/10 mm steel plate welded on
 6 80/80/6 mm steel SHS
 7 34 mm thermally insulated aluminium panel
 8 220 mm steel channel section (RSC)
 9 fluorescent tube
10 12 mm steel plate
11 360 mm steel channel section (UB)
12 plasterboard on supporting structure
13 metal grating
14 heating pipe
15 60 mm dia. tubular steel balustrade post
16 60 mm dia. steel tube
17 12 mm untreated oak on
    18 mm plywood 50 mm screed;
    110 mm filigree floor
18 45 mm aluminium panel
19 200/100/5 mm steel RHS
20 310 mm steel channel section
21 plasterboard, painted grey

Congress Centre in Barcelona

Architect: Carlos Ferrater, Barcelona

The "Palacio de Congressos" is on the south-western outskirts of Barcelona. This area was neglected for a long time, and is now devoted to large complexes including sport and leisure facilities, hotels, banks, offices and the main roads running in and out of the town. Only the Torre Melina gardens in the immediate vicinity of the Congress Centre offer a green urban area that it would be pleasant to spend some time in. The basic cube of this building is articulated to create apertures providing a view of the gardens and at the same time identifies the complex's three principal uses: the auditorium, the exhibition hall with conference rooms above it and the narrow strip accommodating catering facilities and service rooms. This creates facilities that considerably enhance Barcelona's leisure provision; the flexibility of the design means that all kinds of events can be ideally served, and provides a wonderful venue for congresses. The architecture of the building makes a major impact, blending beautifully into its context and perfectly set off by the gardens. The inside of the building is dominated by areas of exposed concrete that give the large, column-free spaces their characteristic charm. The only steel uprights taking up a dialogue with the trees in the park are to be found in the cafeteria, whose floor-to-ceiling windows face the gardens. The internal access areas are illuminated by roof-lights. In the foyer, four roof apertures with different geometry allow light into the space from all directions – the interplay of light and shade emphasizes the cubature of the rooms and bathes the exposed concrete in warm light. The zone between the halls has a system of overlapping continuous window strips; these face north, and break the long, narrow area down into diagonal zones. The large auditorium is the core of the complex and has a total of 2049 seats. The space can be divided into two smaller units by a screen: a ground-floor hall with 1600 seats and a smaller one using the balcony, with 450 seats. Acoustic research contributed to both the shape of the ceilings and the choice of materials used, so that classical concerts, cinema showings and also conferences can be held in the best possible sound conditions. The double-vaulted ceiling with hinged wooden louvres means that the acoustics are uniformly excellent all over the hall. The walls and ceilings are made up of derived timber panels, and these are either overlaid with maple veneer or painted. The auditorium floors are carpeted and the seats upholstered to improve the acoustics. When the full hall is being used, the dividing wall that isolates the gallery "disappears" into a broad shaft in the double ceiling. The shaft makes a considerable impact on the external appearance of the hall, as it protrudes above the otherwise flat roof, giving the building its individual silhouette.

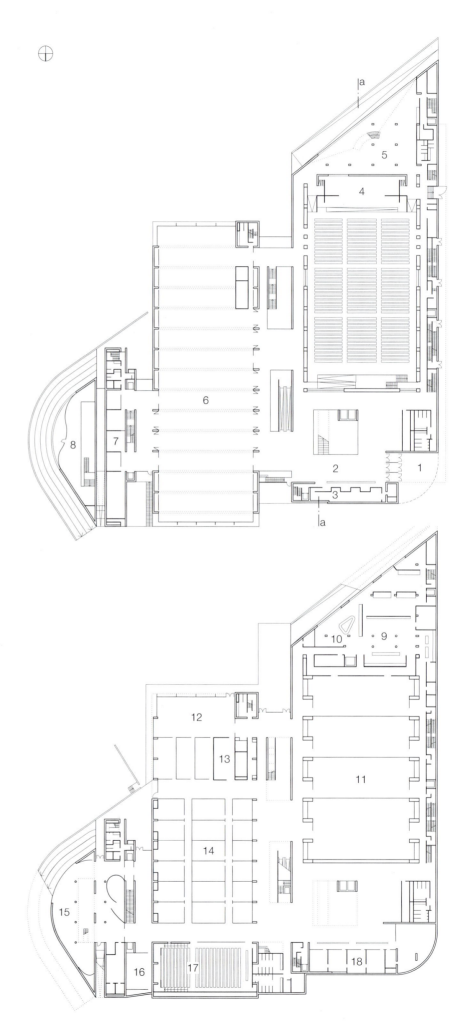

plan entrance level

plan garden level
scale 1:1000

1 entrance
2 hall
3 cloakroom
4 auditorium
5 foyer
6 exhibition hall
7 shop
8 café and restaurant
9 kitchen
10 washing facilities
11 banqueting hall
12 hall
13 store for wall elements
14 room units with
   adjustable wall elements
15 access to café and restaurant
16 multi-purpose room
17 hall with special
   technical equipment
18 side rooms for conferences

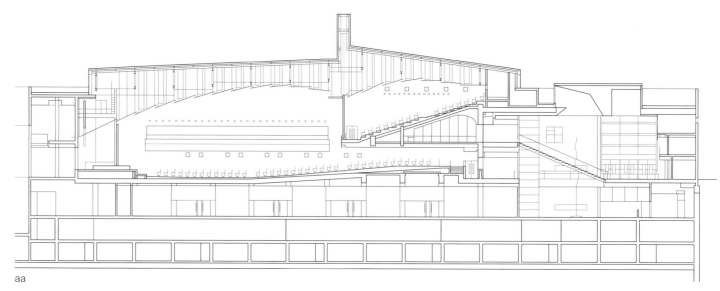

aa

vertical section
scale 1:500
detail section sliding wall
scale 1:20

1 Ø 16 mm traction rope
2 track UPN 300 steel section
3 steel I-column 160 mm deep
4 lighting
5 55/45 squared timber frame

6 12 mm plywood sheet with maple veneer
7 inspection aperture
8 20 mm veneered timber sheet
   frame 50/20 mm steel RHS
   12 mm plasterboard
   120 mm mineral-wool acoustic insulation
   12 mm plasterboard
   74 mm fibreglass
   74 mm steel channel
   2× 12 mm plasterboard

9 40/18 mm solid maple strip
10 supperting structure: 50/20 mm steel RHS,
   20 mm plywood sheet, framed in 100/40 mm
   steel RHS with reflector sheet welded in
11 50/50 mm steel SHS
12 rubber section for sound insulation
   fixed with timber strip
13 142 mm plain wood-strip flooring
   with fabric covering
14 textile curtain

A

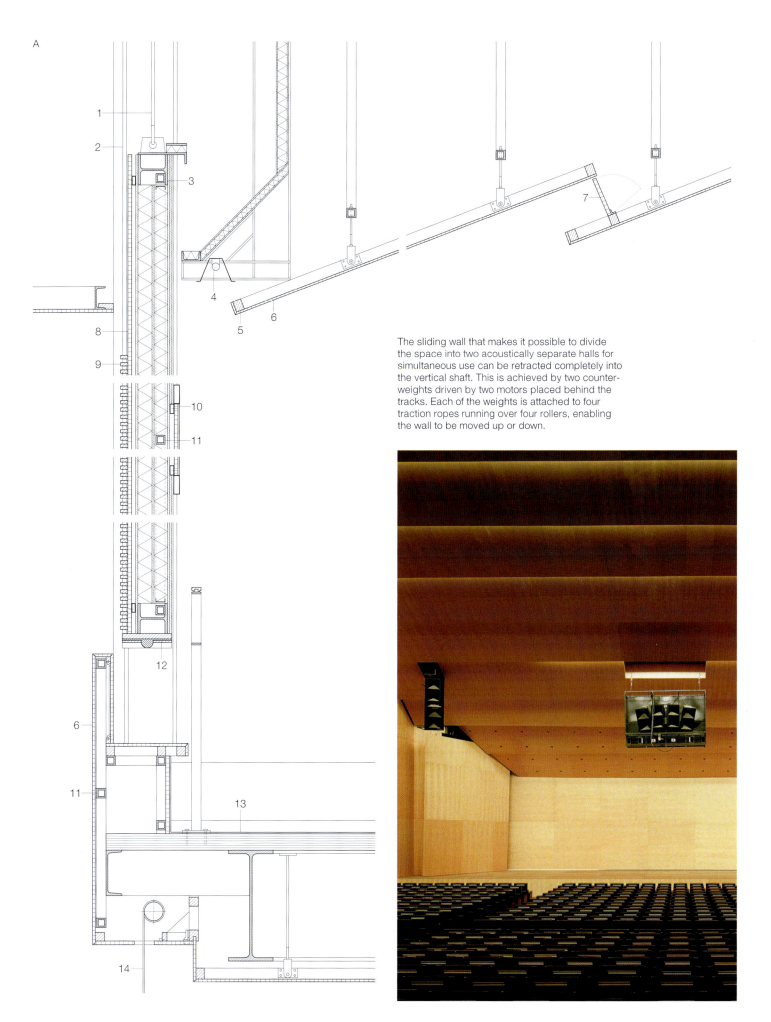

1

2

3

4

5

6

7

8

9

10

11

12

6

11

13

14

The sliding wall that makes it possible to divide the space into two acoustically separate halls for simultaneous use can be retracted completely into the vertical shaft. This is achieved by two counter-weights driven by two motors placed behind the tracks. Each of the weights is attached to four traction ropes running over four rollers, enabling the wall to be moved up or down.

Concert Hall in León

Architects: Mansilla + Tuñón, Madrid

León, which is in north-western Madrid, was once capital of the Castile-León region, to which it gave its name. It has a number of striking churches, and so the architects tried to make the new building fit in with this key feature. The narrow bar-shape of the gallery area and the cuboid clock of the auditorium stand out from the ensemble. The broken facade of the gallery is in white concrete, but the cubic volumes of the auditorium are clad in large white marble slabs. The uniform colour scheme pulls the ensemble together. From the entrance, which is placed at the point where the building volumes intersect, leads visitors into the foyer. From there they move on into the anteroom of the hall. The ground floor houses the storerooms, toilets, dressing-rooms, cloakrooms and a café. The fittings in the auxiliary spaces are all in white-painted concrete and oak, thus seeming plain and functional in contrast with the auditorium, which is clad entirely in dark timber. The hall can seat from 600 to 1200 people – depending on how it is configured. The seats are arranged facing each other with the stage in the centre: the architecture plays with the motto "see and be seen". The succinct interior design derives from the acoustic requirements: the timber envelope consists of large continuous bands whose breadth and orientation change continually. Even the niches in the side walls and the rows of seats are designed to meet technical acoustical criteria. The lighting is built into the wall and ceiling elements, so that that there is no risk of additional fittings spoiling the character of the hall, which is entirely derived from the grain patterns of the dark wood.

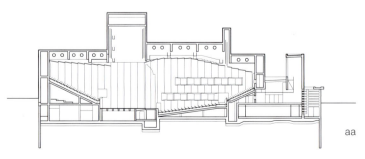

aa

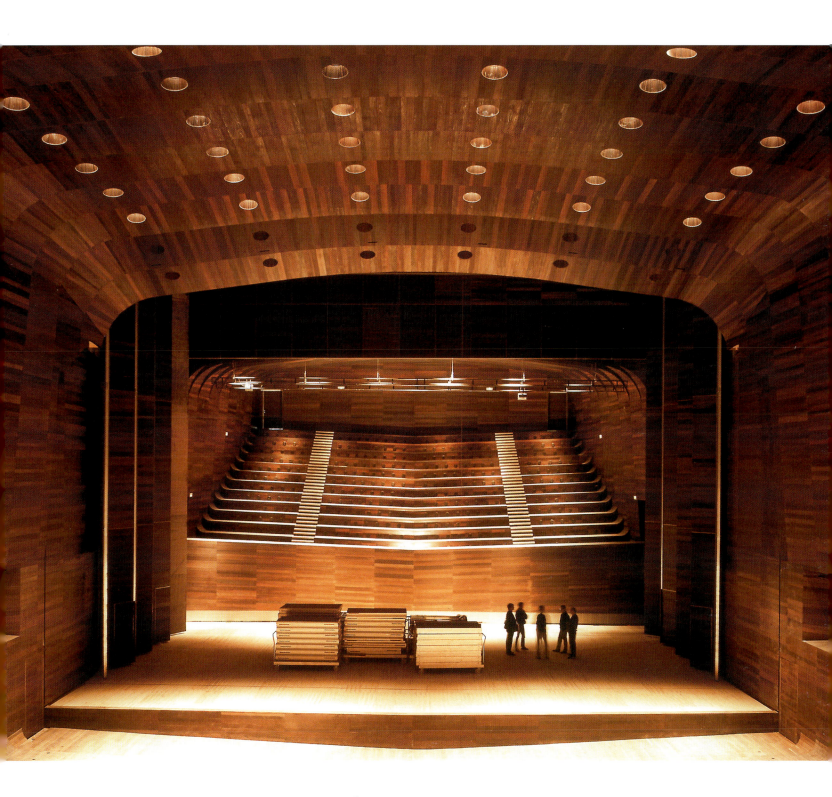

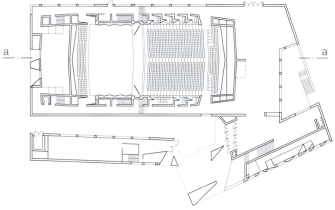

Section
plan
scale 1:1000

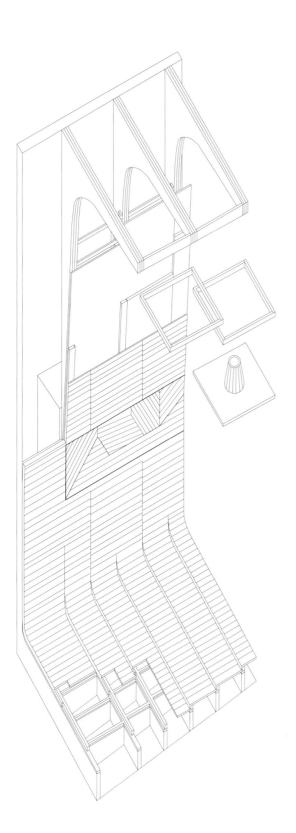

axonometric drawing
section wall cladding
scale 1:10

1 Wall cladding:
   treated wenge veneer
   laminated sheet fireproof,
   thickness dependent on position in hall
   70/30 mm galvanized steel tubes
   inbetween acoustic insulation,
   thickness dependent on position in hall
   15 mm plasterboard,
   in curved areas 2x 6 mm
2 aluminium section
3 prefabricated fireproof
   laminated wood section
4 60/60 mm steel angle
5 white reinforced concrete wall

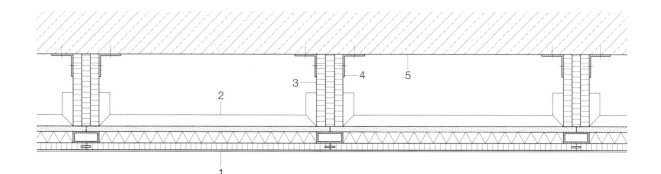

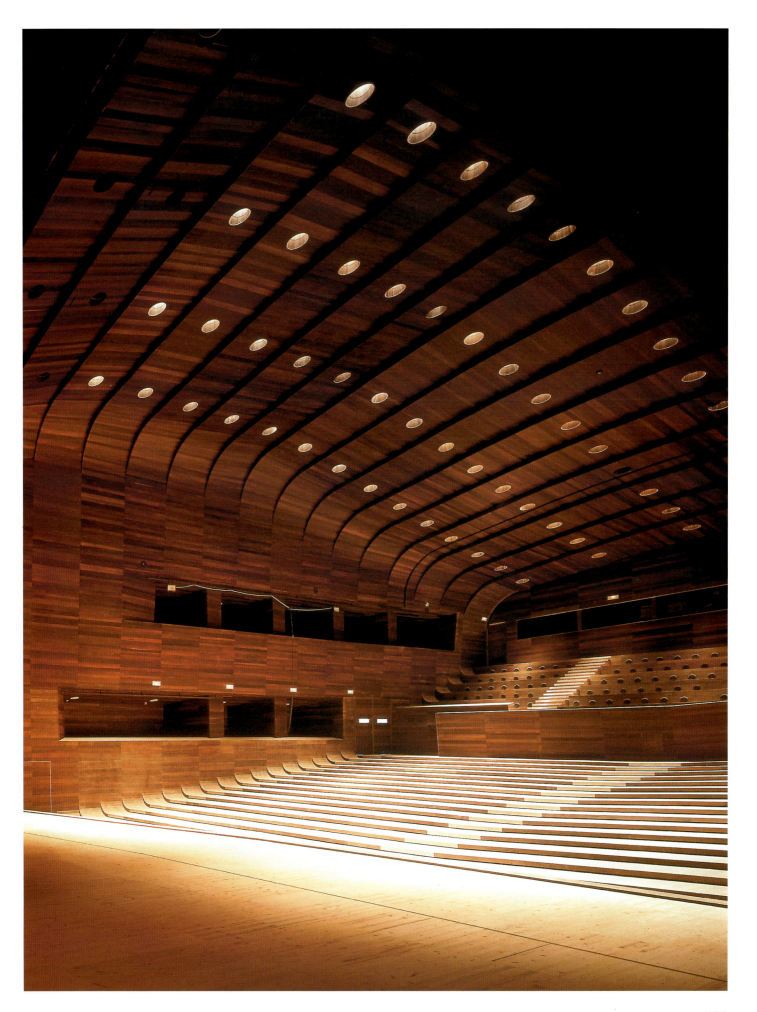

Metropolitan Express, Hamburg – Cologne

Architects: von Gerkan, Marg und Partner, Hamburg

Comfortable leather seats, subdued colours and high-quality materials – if travellers couldn't see the countryside rushing past outside the long windows they might think they were in an exclusive club. The silver-grey Metropolitan carries businessmen from Hamburg to Cologne in only three hours and twenty minutes, making an attractive alternative to driving or flying. The "Metropolitan" runs four times a day in each direction on weekdays, once on Saturday and twice on Sunday. The interior of the train is as revolutionary as the journey concept. Enormous attention has been paid to detail, and no expense has been spared in terms of the ultra-modern comfort offered by the design and the luxury of the materials. Swiss birch veneer, brushed stainless steel, natural textiles and leather: the natural materials used for the interior furnishings and fittings create a dignified atmosphere.

Each train is made up of seven coaches, and passengers have three different zones at their disposal: "Office", "Club" and the "Silence" area, offering workplaces and meeting areas, or the chance of relaxing or having a nap. The seats in the coaches are arranged in rows of three; each seat is 52 cm wide, and thus more comfortable than in the traditional ICE (Inter-City Express) trains. The seats were specially designed for the Metropolitan, and are derived from Charles and Ray Eames's Lounge Chair: a moulded plywood shell is concealed under leather-covered seat upholstery; the height of the leather headrests is individually adjustable. Folding tables are attached to the chair backs, and switches and outlet sockets are built into the armrests and the base. The tables between the facing seats can be folded out as needed, and leather insets stop crockery or writing materials slipping off when the train accelerates or brakes. The luggage rack – like the ceiling covering – is in stainless steel, with slit areas installed in the ceiling for interference-free mobile phone reception. The change of material is marked by visible joints, formed both horizontally and vertically by lengths of stainless steel. The edge of the reflective ceiling covering are coach are floodlit; reading lamps with individual switches complement the lighting for each seat.

Bistro
Open-plan compartment
Ground floor plans · sections
scale 1:50

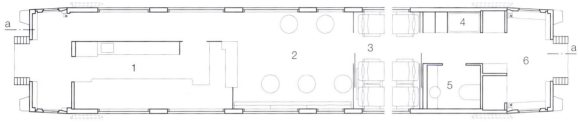

1 On-board kitchen
2 Bistro
3 Open-plan
  compartment
4 Storage space
5 WC
6 Doorway
7 Driver's cab

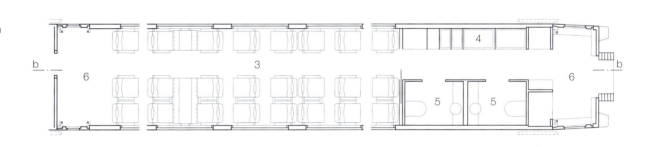

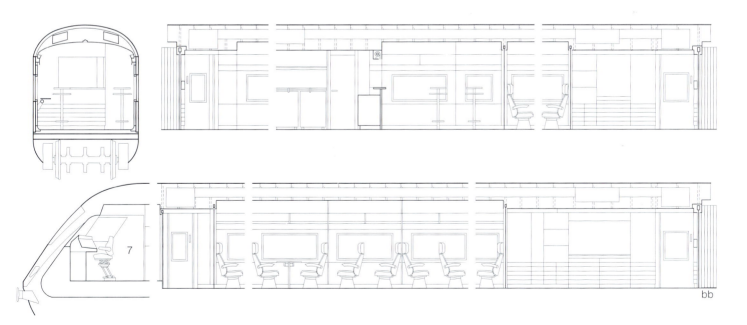

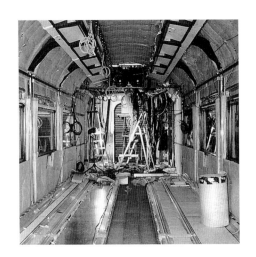

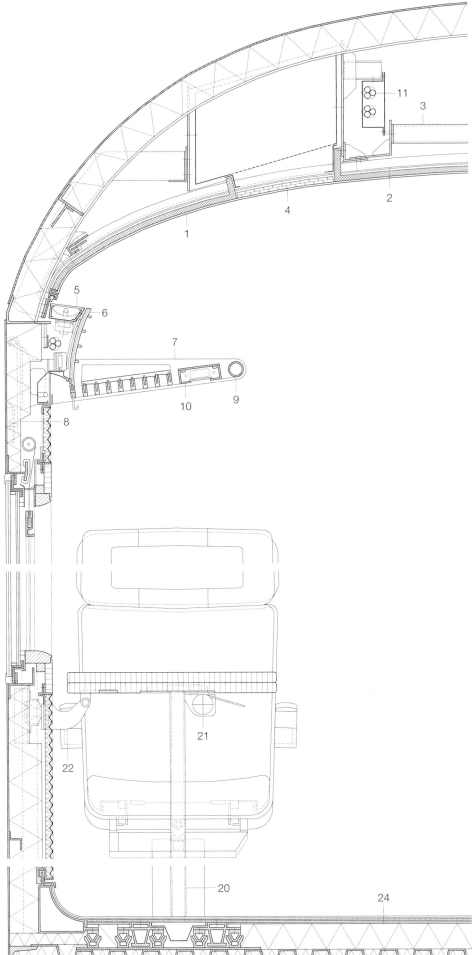

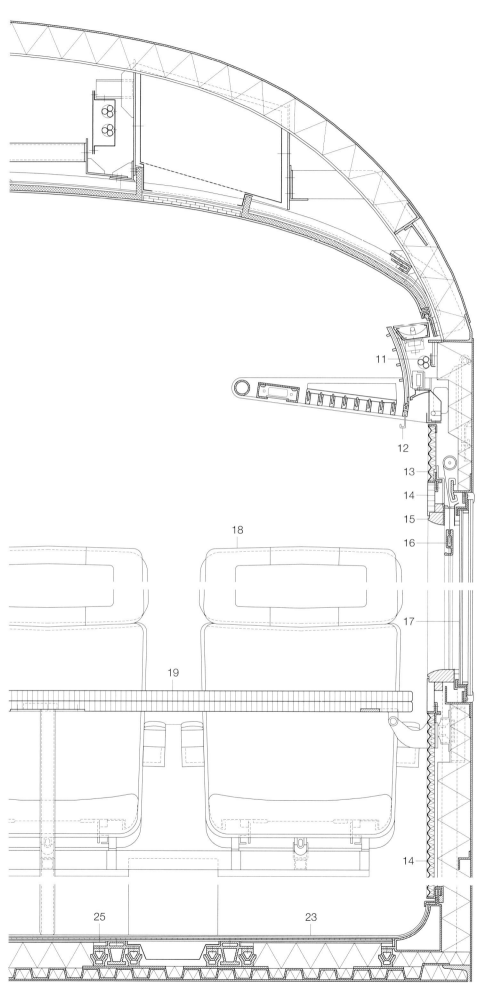

Open-plan
compartment
cross-section
scale 1:10

1 ceiling field 1000 mm,
  ceiling cladding fixed in slide
  bearing on both sides:
  woven stainless steel
  acoustic fleece
  15 mm melamine foam
2 aluminium channel
3 aluminium I-section transverse beam
  welded and bolted to head plate
4 air conditioning outlet
5 ceiling flood, clear glass cover
6 12 mm prefabricated medium-density
  fibreboard wall cladding
7 stainless steel strut screwed to 8
8 10 mm stainless steel end plate
  suspended in 12 mm stainless steel tube
9 42 mm stainless steel tube with
  seat numbers lasered in
10 anodized aluminium section
  with built-in seat lighting
11 cable duct
12 cast stainless steel clothes hook
13 corrugated stainless steel in stainless steel
  section, backed with silicon foam
14 20 mm Swiss birch inspection flap, painted
15 frame timber section,
  veneer Swiss birch, painted
16 anti-dazzle device
17 fixed glazing: double glazing 12 mm
  laminated safety glass + 12 mm cavity +
  8 mm laminated safety glass, inside grid foil
18 Swiss birch prefabricated shell,
  seats leather, edge protector stainless steel
19 table Swiss birch, painted
20 42 mm stainless steel tube
21 revolving fitting stainless steel
22 table-to-wall attachment anodized
  cast aluminium part
23 carpet, woven synthetic fibre,
  laid in three strips, glued
  edge protector section stainless steel
24 2x fibre-glass mats covered with copper foil
25 de-coupling element to absorb vibration on
  rubber-metal bearing

The actual challenge for the designers in terms
of the interior was making the natural materials
used comply with the rigorous safety requirements, which prescribe fireproof, hard-wearing
fittings and furniture, with minimum vibration.
Also, the shapes and constructions chosen must
exclude any chance of injury, and withstand
forces of 5G. To keep the interior as vibration-
and shock-free as possible, the interior fittings
were completely disconnected from the external
steel envelope. Decoupling elements are placed
in the floor and wall area (at luggage-rack level)
to facilitate this tube-in-tube principle. A special
paint was developed for the train. This seals the
surfaces like a melamine coating, making the
veneered areas scratchproof.

"Am Moosfeld"
Underground Station in Munich

Architects: Sturm & Kessler, Munich
Lighting design: Ingo Maurer, Munich

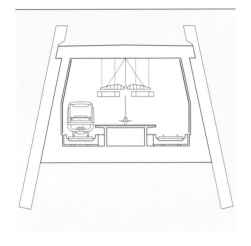

Platform cross-section
scale 1:400

It's highly noticeable even as the train goes through the station: a long run of lettering hugging the slightly curved wall of the underground tunnel, so that the passengers sitting on the train know they're passing through Moosfeld station. On one side the pillar-box red letters catch your attention, and on the other side the wall itself is finished in this colour. The vertical mid-point of the letter is placed precisely on the horizontal kink of the wall, which leans slightly inwards at the top, further emphasizing this fact.

Originally the architects wanted to paint the lettering directly on to the tunnel walls, and the whole station was to be in exposed concrete. But the difficult conditions (the station is built entirely in groundwater) meant cladding the wall with aluminium sections, and then cutting the big letters out of the individual panels. This gave the lettering a three-dimensional depth that makes it seem even more dynamic. In fact the entire station concept aims to give a sense of arrival, of departure, above all of travelling – there are no unnecessary fittings to break up the view – and the subdued stainless steel furniture retreats behind the impression left by the lettering and the lighting, which designed especially for this station. The lampshades are arranged in pairs along the central axis of the curving platform, 80 of them in all. They are set transversely to the platform and pull the long space together visually. The walls and lamps enhance the dynamic impression by emphasizing the curved ground plan.

Lamp
Section
scale 1:20

Wall cladding
Platform
Vertical section
Horizontal section
scale 1:5

1 shell 1 mm lacquered steel outside silver, inside green
2 stainless steel suspension loop
3 58 W fluorescent tube with wide angle protection tube reflector
4 lampholder steel 10/60/1560 mm
5 rib 40/10 mm steel flat
6 M 6 screw lamp fitting
7 35/35/3 mm steel SHS
8 power cable
9 end rib 40/20 mm steel flat

10 powder-coated corrugated aluminium 30/10/1,2 mm
11 50/30/3 mm steel RHS
12 25/25/3 mm steel angle
13 30/70/3 mm steel section
14 80/65/6 mm steel angle
15 steel compensation piece
16 steel anchoring screw
17 reinforced concrete wall

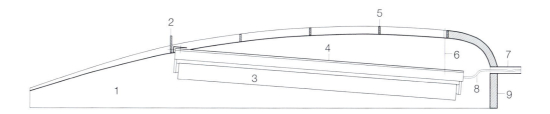

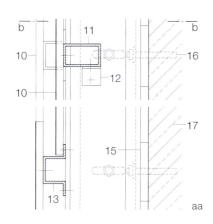

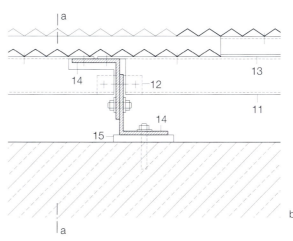

"Westfriedhof"
Underground Station in Munich

Architects: Auer + Weber, Munich
Lighting design: Ingo Maurer, Munich

The first thing passengers see when coming into this underground station is unusual – at first it seems most like a room installation in the sort of off-beat exhibition venue that is popular all over the place nowadays. But the unclad shaft walls and the enormous lampshades are part of the "West-friedhof" underground station. In a similar way to the "Am Moosfeld" station (see p. 164ff.), the architects have cut out any unnecessary decoration, and established the character of the station by reducing the interior fittings to discreet stainless steel furniture, framed by rough concrete walls and ceilings. The gigantic aluminium lampshades are reminiscent of factory hall lighting and yet cancel out this impression at the same time. Their red, blue and yellow internal surfaces act as an appropriate counterweight to the archaic-looking walls. The eleven domes suspended above the platform are each fitted with twelve fluorescent tubes.
The lamps were set as far back in the dome as possible so as not to spoil the "shining" impression made by the shades. Each of the lampshades has a hanging device in the form of a silver-painted steel frame above it; these have blue fluorescent tubes that bathe the rough walls and ceilings in blue light, thus underlining the contrast between the lights and the concrete surfaces around them.

Platform
Cross section
Scale 1:250

Light dome
view from below
cross section
scale 1:50

1 2 mm aluminium dome, painted inside
  with continuous peripheral reinforcement
  20 segments in all
2 25/25/3 mm aluminium reinforcing ring
3 lamp with warm white fluorescent tubes
4 25/25/2.5 mm aluminium rib
5 40/40/4 mm aluminium carrier ring
6 2×40 mm aluminium connecting bracket
  riveted and levelled inside, painted the colour
  of the dome after fitting

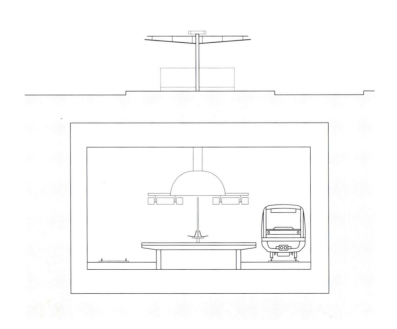

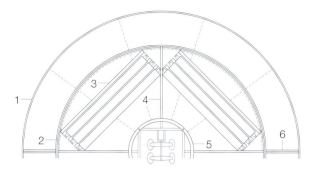

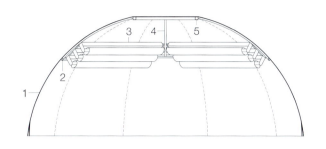

House in Vila Nova

Client:
private
Architect:
Alvaro Siza Vieira, Porto
with:
Luisa Penha and João Pedro Xavier
Interior designers:
Alvaro Siza, Luisa Renha and
Cecilla Cavaca, Porto
Structural engineering:
GOP, Porto
Date: 1994

Alvaro Siza Vierira
Born 1933 in Matoshinhos,
Portugal; studied architecture at
Porto University;
1954 first building commission;
own practice in Porto;
taught at Porto University.

numerous awards and honorary
memberships.

Attic in Vienna

Client:
Andrea and Karl Vass
Architects:
Erich Hubmann & Andreas Vass,
Vienna
with:
Carmen Diez Medina
Structural engineering:
Gmeiner & Haferl, Wien
Timber construction:
Gattringer, Schleibbs
Exposed concrete and building
contractor:
Denk GmbH, Wien
Furniture and joinery:
Obermüller GmbH, Langenlois
Date: 1995

Erich Hubmann
Born 1961 in Dobl, Steirmark; joint
practice with Andreas Vass from
1989; taught at the Akademie der
Bildenden Künste, Vienna from
1992.

Andreas Vass
Born 1961 in Vienna; joint studio
with Erich Hubermann from 1989;
taught at the Akademie der
Bildenden Künste, Vienna from
1992; visiting professorship in
Ferrara, Italy from 1999.

hubmann.vass@akbild.ac.at

Duplex Apartment
in New York

Client:
Peter and Eileen Norton
Architect:
Maya Lin, Maya Lin Studio,
New York with David Hotson,
New York
Structural engineering:
Friedman & Oppenheimer,
New York
Services and technical equipment:
Ivan Pollak, I.P. Group Inc.,
New York
Contractor:
David Giovannitti, Inc., New York
Metal construction:
Kern/Rockenfield,
Inc. (Larry King), New York
Date: 1999

Maya Lin
Born 1959 in Athens, Ohio;
independent Studio since 1986;
1993 Artist in Residence at the
Wexner Center for the Arts, Ohio
and 1994 the Residence at
Pilchuck, Washington; 1998
Resident in Architecture at the
American Academy in Rom;
Lectures at the Smithsonian
Institution, Whitney Museum,
Harvard University, San Francisco
Museum of Modern Art, among
others.

mlinstudio@earthlink.net

House in Ito

Client:
Seiichiro Sekiguchi
Architects:
Motoyoshi Itagaki, Architect and
Associates
with:
Hiromi Sugimoto
Structural engineering:
F.S.K. Structural Design
Consultants, Tokyo
Services and technical equipment:
Tetens Consulting Engineering
Com., Ltd, Tokyo
Date: 1991

Motoyoshi Itagaki
Born 1940 in Hokkaido; grew up in
Tokyo; 1963 graduated from the
Tokyo University of Fine Arts,
Department of architecture; since
1963 member of Isoya Yoshida
Architect & Associates; established
Motoyoshi Itagaki Architect &
Associates in 1977; since 2001
lectures at the Tokyo University of
Fine Arts.

Chapel in Valleacerón

Client:
private
Architect:
Sol Madridejos,
J.C. Sancho Osinaga
with:
Luis Renedo, Juan Antonio Garrido,
Emilio Gómez-Ramos, Patricia
Planell, Marta Toral, Andrey García,
Javier Moreno, Martin Pozullo
Date: 2000

Sol Madridejos
Born 1958 in Madrid; worked with
BAU Architects with J.Carlos
Sancho from 1983; 1997 joint
Sancho-Madridejos practice
founded; 1998 chair at E.T.S.A.M.
Madrid.

J.C.Sancho Osinaga
Born 1958 in San Sebastian;
worked with BAU Architects with
Sol Madridejos from 1983; 1992
doctorate at E.T.S.A.M. Mädrid;
1997 joint Sancho-Madridejos
practice founded.

numerous awards, prizes and
exhibitions.

soljc@iberfin.es

Synagogue in Dresden

Client:
Jewish community in Dresden
Architects:
Wandel, Hoefer, Lorch und Hirsch,
Saarbrücken/Leipzig
Structural engineering:
Schweitzer Ingenieure,
Saarbrücken/Dresden
Services and technical equipment:
Zibell Willner & Partner, Dresden
Lighting design:
Wilms GmbH, Wiesentheid
Acoustics/building physics:
Müller BBM, Dresden
Project management:
Fischer Projektmanagment, Leipzig
Date: 2002

Andrea Wandel
Born 1963 in Saarbrücken.
Hubertus Wandel
Born 1926 in Meseritz, Branden-
burg; various teaching posts.
Dr. Rena Wandel Hoefer
Born 1959 in Saarbrücken.
Andreas Hoefer
Born 1955 in Hamburg.
Prof. Wolfgang Lorch
Born 1960 in Nürtingen/Neckar;
2001 chair at the TH Stuttgart.
Nickolaus Hirsch
Born 1964; taught from 2000 at the
Architectural association in London.

wandel-hoefer-lorch.de

Kindergarten in Lustenau

Client:
Marktgemeinde Lustenau
Architects:
Helmut Dietrich, Much Untertrifaller,
Bregenz
Structural engineers:
Ernst Mader, Markus Flatz, Bregenz
Electrical planning:
Hecht Licht- und Elektroplanung,
Rankweil
Date: 1999

Helmut Dietrich
Born 1957 in Mellau, Austria;
worked in the Studio Paolo Piva in
Biella, Italy from 1983 to 1986;
free-lance from 1986; association
with Much Untertrifaller, Bregenz;
1994 founded Dietrich/Untertrifaller
Architects;
1998 Staatspreis für Tourismus und
Architectur; board member of the
Vorarlberger Architectur Institut
from 2000.

Much Untertrifaller
Born 1959 in Bregenz;
worked in the Much Untertrifaller
sen. practice from 1982 to 1985;
group association with Helmut
Dietrich and Much Untertrifaller sen.
from 1986;
1994 Dietrich/Untertrifaller
Architects founded.

www.dietrich.untertrifaller.com

Fashion Boutique in Munich

Client:
Michael and Rosy Maendler
Architects:
Petzinka Pink Architects,
Düsseldorf
with:
Andreas Jablonski, Michael Marx
Interior design:
Ladenbau Schmidt, Würzburg
Services and technical equipment:
Ebert Ingenieure, Munich
Electrics/lighting:
Elan, Lightings- und Elektroanlagen
GmbH, Cologne
Date: 1997

Thomas Pink
Born 1958 in Hamburg;
1980 to 1985 scientific assistant at
the RWTH Aachen under Prof.
J.Kohl; free-lance architect with
Kleinhues, Rorup und Döring,
Düsseldorf from 1985; 1994
founded practice with Karl-Heinz
Petzinka.

Karl-Heinz Petzinka
Born 1956 in Bocholt; worked with
O.M. Ungers from 1982 to 1983;
1983 to 1985 assistant at the
RWTH Aachen under Prof. Döring;
1994 founded practice Thomas
Pink; 1994 chair at the
TU Darmstadt.

www.petzinka-pink.de

Jewellery Gallery in Munich

Client:
Isabella Hund
Architects:
Landau + Kindelbacher, Munich
Project partner:
Lene Jünger
Building contractor and
dry construction:
Marcel Dittrich Bauunternehmung,
Munich
Joinery, metalwork and glazing:
Möbel Bauer, Altötting
Floor coating:
Unger Thermoboden,
Unterschleißheim
Natural stone work:
Granit & Marmor Galerie, Gilching
Date: 1997

Gerhard Landau
Born 1965 in Rodalben;
1992 founded practice in Munich;
1993 partnership with Kindelbacher; various teaching posts.
Ludwig Kindelbacher
Born 1965 in Munich;
1993 partnership with Landau;
2000 to 2001 taught at the FH
Rosenheim.

numerous exhibitions and prizes.

www.landaukindelbacher.de

Shop and Spa in New York

Client:
Hiroko Sueyoshi Planners
Architects:
ARO (Architectural Research
Office); Stephen Cassal,
Adam Yarinsky, New York
Project architect:
Scott Abrahams
with:
Josh Pulver, Eunice Seng,
Rosalyne Shieh, Kim Yao
Art Director Shiseido:
Aoshi Kudo
Project designer Shiseido:
Rikya Uekusa
Structural engineering:
Selnick/Harwood
Services and technical equipment:
Lilker Associates
Lighting design:
Johnson Schwinghammer, Inc.
Curtain design:
Mary Bright, Inc.
Audio-visual concept:
Shen Milsom and Wilke
Date: 2000

ARO practice founded in 1993 by
Stephen Cassell and Adam
Yarinsky; both partners have held
various teaching posts.

www.aro.net

Fashion Boutique in Vienna

Client:
Don Gil AG
Architects:
propeller z; Korkut Akkalay, Kabru,
Kriso Leinfellner, Philipp Tschofen,
Carmen Wiederin, Vienna
Statics:
werkraum_wien
Building management:
Buchegger & Schmutzenhofer
Lighting:
Christian Ploderer/VEST
Acoustics:
David Heigner
Date: 2000

1994 propeller z practice founded;
numerous competitions.

www.propellerz.at

Fashion Shop in London

Client:
Marni
Architects:
Future Systems, London
with:
Jan Kaplicky, Amanda Levete,
Matthew Heywood, Angus Pond,
Rachel Stevenson
Structural engineering:
Ove Arup & Partners, London
Main contractor:
Purple Shopfitters, London
Stainless steel work:
Marzorati Ronchetti, Cantu, Italy
Glazing:
Compass Glass + Glazing,
Unit 29, London
Interior finish:
Liquid Plastics, Astral House,
Lanca-shire
Date: 2000

Jan Kaplicky
Born 1937 in Prague; since1969
independent architect; since 1989
office partnership with Amanda
Levete.
Amanda Levete
Born 1955 in Bridgend, UK; 1982
Diploma Architectural Association,
London; since 1980 independent
architect; since 1989 office
partnership with Jan Kaplicky.

www.future-systems.com

Supermarket in Wattens

Client:
MPreis WarenvertriebsGmbH, Völs
Architects:
Dominique Perrault, Paris;
Rolf Reichert, Architects RPM,
Munich
Site supervision:
MPreis WarenvertriebsGmbH,
Bernhard Schiendl
with:
MPreis: Hans Efferl
RPM: Bernd Greger
Dominique Perrault:
Mathias Fritsch, Cyril Lancelin,
Gaëlle Lauriot-Prévost,
Ralf Levedag
Structural engineering:
Guy Morisseau, Paris;
Alfred Brunnsteiner, Natters
Lighting design:
HG Engineering, Innsbruck
Services and technical equipment:
Tivoliplan, Innsbruck
Date: 2000

Dominique Perrault
Born 1953 in Clermont-Ferrand;
own practice from1981; numerous
prizes and publications.

www.perraultarchitecte.com
www.RPM-ARCHITEKTEN.de

Eat in/Take out Restaurant in Tokyo

Client:
Best Bridal Co.Ltd
Architects:
Klein Dytham architecture;
Astrid Klein, Mark Dytham Hiroto
Kubo, Tokyo
Main contractor:
D. Brain Co.Ltd
Date: 2000

Astrid Klein
Born 1962 in Varese, Italy; Klein
Dytham architecture practice
founded in 1990;
1997 teaching post at Nihon
University, College of Science and
Technology.

Mark Dytham
Born 1964 in Northamptonshire,
England; Klein Dytham architecture
practice founded in 1990;
2000 teaching post at Tokyo
Science University.

www.klein-dytham.com

Brasserie in New York

Client:
Restaurant Associates
Architects:
Diller + Scofidio, New York,
Elisabeth Diller, Ricardo Scofidio
with: Charles Rentro (Project
leader), Deane Simpson
Structural engineering:
Alan Burden Structural Environ-
ment, Tokyo
Services and technical equipment:
T+M Associates, Middletown,
New Jersey
Lighting:
Richard Shaver, New York
Multi Media:
Scharff Weisberg, New York
Main contractor:
Construction by Design,
Hauppage, NY
Date: 2000

Elizabeth Diller
works as professor of architecture
at Princeton University.

Ricardo Scofidio
works as professor of architecture
at the Cooper Union.

numerous exhibitions and
publications

disco@dillerscofidio.com

Bar in Heidelberg

Client:
Print Media Lounge GmbH;
G. Fanton, G. Niedermair
Architects:
Liquid Architectur/Landschaft
Dung, Radmacher, Schultz, Schulz
Statics:
Wagner+Zeitter, Wiesbaden
Interior finishing:
Heikaus GmbH, Pleidelsheim
Lighting: ZipLight, Heidelberg
Counter construction:
Fa.Wolf, Heidelberg
Glazing:
Ehrmann GmbH, Eppelheim
Date: 2001

Andrea Dung
Born 1968; studied at the TU
Darmstadt, diploma 1997.
Edmund Radmacher
Born 1966; studied landscape
architecture in Florence;
diploma 1995.
Kerstin Schultz
Born 1967; studied at the TU
Darmstadt, diploma 1997.
Werner Schulz
Born 1966; studied at the TU
Darmstadt, diploma 1997.

liquid_architekten@t-online.de

Office Bar in Tokyo

Client:
AMP Japan
Architects:
Klein Dytham architecture; Astrid
Klein, Mark Dytham; Tokyo
Main contractor:
D. Brain Co. Ltd
Date: 2001

Astrid Klein
Born 1962 in Varese, Italy; Klein
Dytham architecture practice
founded in 1990;
1997 teaching post at Nihon
University, College of Science and
Technology.

Mark Dytham
Born 1964 in Northamptonshire,
UK; Klein Dytham architecture
practice founded in 1990;
2000 teaching post at Tokyo
Science University.

www.klein-dytham.com

Architects' Office in Berlin

Client:
Nietz Prasch Sigl Tchoban Voss
Architects BDA, Hamburg, Berlin,
Dresden
Architects:
Nietz Prasch Sigl Tchoban Voss
Architects BDA, Berlin;
Sergei Tchoban
Project manager:
Daniel Brand
Steel construction for stairs:
Rainer Mantel, Bad Karlshafen
Glazing:
Hiesinger, with Metallbau Burhop,
both Berlin
Date: 2001

Wolfang Nietz
Born 1941 in Hamburg.
Alf M. Prasch
Born 1941 in Görlitz/Silesia.
Peter Sigl
Born 1934 in Hamburg.
Sergei Tchoban
Born 1962 in St. Petersburg,
Russia.
Ekkehard Voss
Born 1963 in Euskirchen, Germany.

present practice association
from 1995

mail@nps-partner-b.de

Agency in Munich

Client:
KMS Designbüro, Munich
Architect:
lynx architecture, Munich
Susanne Muhr, Volker Petereit
working with tools off. architecture;
Andreas Notter, Eva Durant
with:
Dirk Härle
Date: 2001

Susanne Muhr
Born 1962;
own practice from 1994;
1995 partnership with Volker
Petereit;
2001 lynx architecture founded.

Volker Petereit
Born 1962;
1995 partnership with Susanne
Muhr;
2001 lynx architecture founded.

www.lynx-a.com

Royal Library in Copenhagen

Client:
Danish Ministry of Culture,
Royal Library
Architects/ landscape architects:
Arkitekterne MAA Schmidt,
Hammer & Lassen K/S
Structural engineering, services
and technical equipment:
Moe & Brødsgaard A/S
Elektrical fittings:
Hansen & Henneberg A/S
Geotechnics:
Hostrup-Schultz & Sørensen A/S
Acoustics:
Anders Chr. Gade
Date: 1999

Morten Schmidt
Born 1956; architect from 1982.
Bjarne Hammer
Born 1955; architect from 1982.
John Foldbjerg Lassen
Born 1953; architect from 1983.
Kim Holst Jensen
Born 1964; architect from 1991.

www.shl.dk

National Library in Paris

Client:
Ministère de Culture
Architect:
Dominique Perrault, Paris
Interior design:
tables/shelves:
Bel S.A., Saint Jean de la Ruelle
Dennery, Alfortville
Bredy S.A., Saint Ouen
Sitraba/Dezellus, Grigny
Furnishings:
Bel S.A., Saint Jean de la Ruelle
Dennery, Alfortville
Martin Stoll, Waldshut-Tiengen
Philips Eclairage, Ivry-sur-Seine
Metal grids:
Euroslot, Scorbe-Clairvaux-F.
Wire gauze:
GKD-Gebrüder Kufferath, Düren
Reading chairs:
Martin Stoll, Waldshut-Tiengen
Lamps/table lamps:
Philips Eclairage, Ivry-sur-Seine
Date: 1995

Dominique Perrault
Born 1953 in Clermont-Ferrand;
own practice from1981; numerous
prizes and publications; teaching
posts include the Escola Tècnica
Superior d'Arquitectura in
Barcelona, Spain, and the ETH in
Zurich.

www.perraultarchitecte.com

Tate Modern in London

Client:
Tate Gallery
Architects:
Herzog & de Meuron, Basel
Associate Architect:
Sheppard Robson + Partners,
London
Structural engineering:
Ove Arup & Partners, London
Facade:
Bug AluTechnic AG, Kent
Steel construction:
Glentworth Fabrications,
Wokingham
Date: 2000

Jacques Herzog
Born 1950 in Basel, Switzerland;
1978 partnership with Pierre de
Meuron; various visiting profes-
sorships from 1983, professor at the
ETH in Zurich from 1999.
Pierre de Meuron
Born 1950 in Basel, Switzerland;
1978 partnership with Jacques
Herzog; various visiting profes-
sorships from 1989; professor at the
ETH in Zurich from 1999.
since 1991 partnership with Harry
Gugger; since 1994 with Christine
Binswanger.
numerous awards, including the
Pritzker Prize in 2001.

info@herzogdemeuron.ch

Congress Centre in Barcelona

Client:
Barcelona Projects, SA
Architects:
Carlos Ferrater Lambarri,
Barcelona
Carlos Ferrater, José Ma Cartañá
Technischer Architect:
Rafael Alabernia
with:
Alberto Peñín
Contractor:
Ferrovial – Agroman
Structural engineering:
Servicios técnicos Agroman;
Antonio Carrasco,
Juan Calvo – Pondio Ingenieros
Acoustics:
Higini Arau
Furniture/fittings:
Euroamykasa; Alfonso Soteres,
Fawaz Kayhali
Date: 2000

Carlos Ferrater
Born 1944 in Barcelona; own
practice from 1971; various
teaching posts from 1987.

ferrater@coac.net

Concert Hall in León

Client:
Ayuntamiento de la Ciudad
de León
Architects:
Mansilla+Tuñón, Arquitectos,
Madrid;
Luis M. Mansilla, Emilio Tuñón
Project management:
Juan Carlos Corona,
Santiago Hernán
with:
Andrés Regueiro Morado,Fernando
García Pino, María Linares
Structural engineering:
Ove Arup & Partners, London
Services and technical equipment:
JG Asociados
Acoustics:
Higini Arau
Contractor:
Auditorio de Leon UTE
Date: 2002

Luis M. Mansilla
Born 1959 in Madrid; various
teaching posts from 1986.

Emilio Tuñón
Born 1958 in Madrid;
teaching from 1986.

circo@wanadoo.es

**Metropolitan Express,
Hamburg – Cologne**

Client:
Dt. Bahn AG
Architects:
gmp Architeken, Hamburg
Design:
Meinhard von Gerkan,
Jürgen Hillmer
with:
Susan Krause, Frank Hülsmeyer,
Maja Gorges, Kristina Kaib,
Bernd Stehle, Torsten Neeland
Interior finishing:
Deutsche Werkstätten Hellerau,
Dresden, Fa. Gartner,
Gundelfingen
Lighting design:
Conceptlicht Angerer
Date: 1999

Meinhard von Gerkan
Born 1935 in Riga; partnership with
Volkwin Marg from 1965;
professor in Braunschweig from
1974; international visiting
professorships.

Jürgen Hillmer
Born 1959 in Mönchengladbach;
with GMP from 1988; partner at
GMP from 1998.

www.gmp-architekten.de

**„Am Moosfeld" Underground
Station in Munich**

Client:
Landeshauptstadt Munich,
represented by the
U-Bahn committee
Architects:
Sturm & Kessler, Munich
Michael Sturm, Manfred Kessler
with:
Dietrich Focke, Kristina Viermetz,
Birgit Bernhöft, Cornelia
Probstmeier
Structural engineering:
Sturm & Kessler, Munich
Shell planning:
Baureferat U-Bahn-Bau,
Abt. Architectur, Munich
Lighting design:
Ingo Maurer GmbH, Munich
Date: 1999

Michael Sturm
free-lance from 1968; partnership
with Manfred Kessler from 1994.

Manfred Kessler
free-lance from 1971; partnership
with Michael Sturm from 1994.

info@sturm-kessler.de

**„Westfriedhof" Underground
Station in Munich**

Client:
Landeshauptstadt Munich,
represented by the U-Bahn
committee Architects:
Auer + Weber, Munich
with: Stephan Suxdorf, Martina
Hornhardt, Heiner Reimers
Shell:
Paul Kramer,
U-Bahn committee Munich
Lighting design:
Ingo Maurer GmbH, Munich
with: Ingo Maurer, Martin Deggel-
mann, Mathias Liedtke,
Gerd Pfarré, Johannes Schmid
Structural engineering:
Mayr + Ludescher, Munich
with: Christoph Naleppa
Date: 1998

Fritz Auer
Born 1933 in Tübingen;
Auer + Weber practice association
from 1980; various professorships
from 1985.

Carlo Weber
Born 1934 in Saarbrücken; Auer +
Weber practice association from
1980; teaching from 1980.

Ingo Maurer
Born 1932 on Reichenau/ Lake
Constance; numerous prizes

www.auer-weber.de
www.ingo-maurer.com

Authors

Christian Schittich (editor)

Born 1956
Studied architecture at University of Technology, Munich,
followed by seven years' office experience and work as
author
from 1991: member of editorial team of DETAIL,
Review of Architecture
from 1992: co-editor
since 1998: sole editor

Christoph Hölz

Born 1962
Studied art history in Munich and Vienna
Academic assistant at the Zentralinstitut für Kunstgeschichte
in Munich from 1988
Publications on 19th and 20th century architectural history
Responsible editor for art book publications

Gerhard Landau

Born 1965 in Rodalben
1992 founded practice in Munich
1993 partnership with Kindelbacher,
various teaching posts.

Ludwig Kindelbacher

Born 1965 in Munich
1993 partnership with Landau,
2000 to 2001 taught at the FH Rosenheim

Illustration credits

The authors and editor wish to extend their sincere thanks to all those who helped to realize this book by making illustrations available. All drawings contained in this volume have been specially prepared in-house. Photos without credits are from the architects' own archives or the archives of "DETAIL, Review of Architecture". Despite intense efforts, it was not possible to identify the copyright owners of certain photos and illustrations. Their rights remain unaffected, however, and we request them to contact us.

From photographers, photo archives and picture agencies:
· Archives d'Architecture Moderne, Brussels: 2.2
· Archiv Margarete Schütte-Lihotzky an der Universität für angewandte Kunst, Vienna: 2.6
· Bagué Trias de Bes, Alejo, Sant Just Desvern: pp. 148–151, 153
· Bibliothèque Royale de Belgique, Brussels: 2.3
· Bildarchiv Foto Marburg, Marburg: 2.4
· Brigola, Victor, Stuttgart: pp. 120–123
· Centraal Museum Utrecht, Rietveld-Schröder Archief, Utrecht: 2.10
· Cook, Peter/View, London: p. 141
· Couturier, Stéphane/Archipress, Paris: 1.5
· Davies, Richard, London: pp. 92–94
· Denancé, Michel/Archipress, Paris: pp. 129, 130–131
· Den Oudsten, Frank, Amsterdam: p. 16 (2.1)
· Fessy, Georges, Paris: pp. 128, 132–137
· Freeman, Reid, New York: p. 84
· Gieshoidt, Martin and Lorusso, Romano, Baureferat Munich: pp. 164, 165
· Gilbert, Dennis/View, London: p. 145
· Glover, Richard/View, London: 1.2
· Graubner, Claus, Berlin: pp. 118, 119
· Halbe, Roland, Stuttgart: pp. 70, 73 top and bottom, 96–98
· Heinrich, Michael, Munich: 3.3, 3.4, 3.11, 3.12, 3.13, pp. 80–83
· Holzherr, Florian, Munich: p. 30 (3.1)

· Ingo Maurer GmbH, Munich: pp. 166–169
· Joseph, David, New York: 3.6, pp. 85, 87
· Laabs, Peter, Dresden: p. 162
· Landecy, Jean-Michel, Geneva: p. 139
· Leith, Marcus, London: p. 147
· Linden, John Edward, Marina Del Rey/CA: 3.16
· Linke, Armin, Milan: 3.18
· MAK – Österreichisches Museum für angewandte Kunst, Vienna: 2.7
· Malagamba, Duccio, Barcelona: pp. 47, 48, 50, 51
· Martinez, Ignacio, A-Hard: pp. 74–77
· Metropolitan Express Train GmbH, Bad Homburg: p. 158
· Miralles Sambola, Jordi, Barcelona: p. 152
· MoMA, New York: 2.15
· Moran, Michael, New York: 1.7, 1.9, pp. 106–111
· Müller-Naumann, Stefan, Munich: 3.8, 3.9, 3.14
· Ott, Thomas, Mühltal: pp. 112–115
· Piazza, Matteo, Milan: 1.6
· Plummer, Henry, Champaign/IL: p. 8 (1.1)
· Richter, Ralph/Architekturphoto, Düsseldorf: 3.7
· Richters, Christian, Münster: 1.10, p. 146 top
· Riehle, Tomas/artur, Cologne: pp. 78, 79
· Scharoun-Archiv, Sammlung Baukunst, Akademie der Künste, Berlin: 2.16
· Schiller, Eric, New York: 1.3, 1.4, pp. 58, 59
· Schink, Hans-Christian/Punctum, Leipzig: pp. 159, 160, 161 top right
· Schittich, Christian, Munich: 1.11, pp. 138, 144
· Shinkenchiku-sha, Tokyo: pp. 63, 64, 142–143
· Spiluttini, Margherita, Vienna: pp. 88–91, 146 bottom
· Štecha, Pavel, Černošice: 2.18
· Suzuki, Hisao, Barcelona: 3.17, pp. 66–69, 154, 155, 157
· Takayama, Kozo, Tokyo: pp. 101–105, 116, 117
· Utimpergher, Paolo, Milan: pp. 52, 53, 55
· Warchol, Paul, New York: pp. 56, 57, 60
· Willebrand, Jens, Cologne: 1.8

From books and journals:
· Boesiger, W./Stonorov, O. (ed.), Le Corbusier et Pierre Jeanneret Œuvre complète 1910–1929. Zurich 1964 (p. 153): 2.12
· Heinz, Thomas A., Frank Lloyd Wright – Interiors and Furniture. London 1994 (p. 70): 2.5
· Le Corbusier – Mein Werk. Stuttgart 1960 (p. 66 top right): 2.11
· Mies van der Rohe – Möbel und Bauten in Stuttgart, Barcelona, Brno. Mailand, 1998 (p. 194): 2.14
· Zabalbeascoa, Anatxu, Houses of the Century. Barcelona, 1998: 2.20

Dust-jacket photo:
Tate Modern in London
Architects:
Herzog & de Meuron, Basle
Photo: Shinkenchiku-sha, Tokyo